The Rare Coin Estate Handbook

By
James L. Halperin
R. Steven Ivy
Gregory J. Rohan

Will Rossman, Editor

IvyPress, Inc.

Dallas, Texas

IvyPress, Inc.

TABLE OF CONTENTS

FOREWORD by Will Rossman, Editor

Introduction

PART 1   Administering Your Collection

PART 2   Estate Planning For Your Collection

PART 3   Evaluating Your Collection

PART 4   Disposing Of Your Collection

APPENDICES

FOREWORD

Tragedy follows no timetable. While editing this handbook, my life was devastated by the sudden loss of my wife, Terri, who unexpectedly suffered a cerebral hemorrhage and died just a week past her 52nd birthday. If you have not experienced the catastrophic loss of a loved one, I'm not sure that there are words to clearly project the modification your perspective undergoes.

I reread the platitudes of the introduction. Those words had seemed powerful and all encompassing just a few short days before – now they were almost empty phrases when measured against the reality we were previously addressing in the abstract. They came nowhere near describing the gamut of feelings that people experience in that situation: shock, disbelief, guilt, fear, grief, and even anger. They say it differs with each person, but I can guarantee that while riding this emotional roller coaster, you are totally unprepared to deal with the minutiae of life... or an ill-planned estate.

We were blessed to have a Will in place, and even with that, the need to hire counsel and petition the Court to "keep" that which I believed to be mine is both a shock and a trial. Without the Will, the process would be three to five times as long and an equal multiple more expensive. If there was a coin collection at issue, I can't imagine the additional burden, but I doubt I could deal with it.

We have tried hard to avoid seeming alarmist in producing this handbook. It can be uncomfortable to even consider that we don't know the number of days we will be blessed with. Now, however, I feel constrained to suggest that if your affairs—numismatic or otherwise—are not in order, you should be alarmed... for the sake of the family you will leave behind.

Please... put your affairs in order. Take it from me – you can live with a Will – and you definitely don't want to die without one!

Will Rossman, Editor

THE RARE COIN ESTATE HANDBOOK

Introduction

We can grant our heirs no greater kindness than to leave our affairs in good order through thoughtful estate planning. If we're fortunate enough to have built an estate, we can leave this earth comfortable in the knowledge that those we love are provided for... but only if we take the time to learn the process and plan for the inevitable.

Your coin collection is an important part of your estate regardless of value, because of the complications involved in evaluating it for probate. The issues of identification, basis, authenticity, grade, markets and timing are often challenging for even the most astute collector, much less any non-collector heirs. Even many probate attorneys are unfamiliar with the breadth of expertise necessary to address all the issues. When these conditions merge, the odds of an unhappy outcome – anything from an unnecessarily high estate tax bill, unreasonable expectations among heirs, or a below-market disposition of the collection – increase exponentially with each element addressed (or neglected!) in ignorance.

The key to estate planning for rare coin collections is in knowing your options. No two individual situations are exactly the same, but they all share common elements. Know what the issues are and who can help you resolve them, and you're well on your way to a satisfactory outcome.

The purpose of this handbook is to identify and explain the issues and options. We're into our fifth decade of appraising, buying, selling, and auctioning rare coins. Over the years, we've encountered virtually every situation imaginable, and have served tens of thousands of clients. The information provided here is the sum product of those experiences, and we offer it for your benefit.

Our sole intention is to provide you with choices and the right questions to ask. Many of the issues addressed may be legal in nature and the statutes covering them will vary somewhat depending on your location. We are in the coin business and as such, do not provide legal advice, nor do we advocate any specific option in this handbook. Please seek competent legal counsel to advise you on which options best suit your individual situation and needs.

Finally, we acknowledge that some readers may be heirs themselves. If so, please accept our condolences on your loss. At this point, some of the options outlined in this handbook are no longer available to you, but the balance of them remain equally valid and doubly important. Ask questions and weigh your options carefully. NOTE: Many of the chapters will contain a "TIPS FOR HEIRS" section at the end that offers suggestions in case you have inherited a coin collection with little or no previous guidance provided.

Regardless of circumstance, good planning will take some of the sting out of an unhappy event. In summation, the road to a successful outcome employs a simple formula:

1. Know the issues.

2. Analyze your personal situation.

3. Qualify your professional assistance.

4. Make informed decisions.

It is our sincere hope that this book will help you plan for the orderly sale of your coin collection, or, if you've inherited a coin collection, that it will guide you through an unfamiliar process.

Production assistance provided by Bob Korver, Cathy Hadd, Carl Watson, Jody Garver and Marsha Taylor.

PART 1
ADMINISTERING YOUR COLLECTION

CHAPTER 1 - RECORD KEEPING

"The longest journey begins with a single step... and a record."

Nobody knows your collection as well as you do. The hours you have spent or will spend enjoying it give you a familiarity that no one else can ever match. As such, no one is more qualified to record your activities than you are. Creating a permanent record for your collection can be either an easy task or a daunting one. While we're sure that the quote below the title of this chapter was created for some other circumstance, there are definite parallels. If you begin an inventory with the first purchase and continue to build it on a "log as you go" basis, the task will not be onerous, and either you or your heirs (or both) will be rewarded when the journey is done. This is the best solution because the time spent with each transaction is minimal, the information is fresh, and a pattern of activity is started that will become habit as your collection develops.

Handwritten or Computer Generated – The Choice Is Yours

The important thing is that you create an inventory of your collection. The method you use to accomplish this is a matter of personal preference. Most coin collectors love numbers and statistics, and may take some additional pleasure in having a well-organized record. This may well take the form of a hand-written ledger, with each item and its history meticulously entered across the columns. Please be honest with yourself, however. If your handwriting is sometimes indecipherable even to you, please consider how difficult (if not impossible) it would be for your heirs to try to decipher those illegible entries and guess at your intent. In this rapidly advancing age of computers and software programs, help is available. Many computer software programs are being written to assist in keeping rare coin inventories. One nifty little example is in production from Collector Technologies, Inc. They can be reached at 106 Orchard St., Belmont, MA 02478-2940. Their toll-free phone number is 1-877-222-6711 or locally, call 617-489-7540. They can also be reached by e-mail at info@abacoin.com.

If you are somewhat computer literate and either dislike packaged programs or don't want all the "bells and whistles," you can create your own record-keeping file on any spreadsheet program like Microsoft® EXCEL. If you use either a manual record or create your own computer file, you need to include at a minimum, the following information:

NECESSARY ITEMS – If creating your own computer file, each of these items should be posted in a separate column to allow easy categorical sorting.

- **PURCHASE DATE**

- **DATE**

- **MINTMARK**

- **DENOMINATION**

- **VARIETY** (If Applicable)

- **GRADE**
  If you are recording uncertified coins, please consider that your heirs will be inclined to accept your opinion as gospel. If you "stretch," you will both overvalue your collection for estate tax purposes and make it virtually impossible for your heirs to be comfortable with any disposition option.

- **GRADING SERVICE** (If Applicable)

- **CERTIFICATE ID NUMBER** (If Applicable)
  This is the inventory number assigned by the grading service and found on the grading label of the holder. It provides coin-specific identification where the collection has multiple items and is valuable as a recovery tool in the unfortunate event that the collection was stolen. If you have a software package that does not include this option, you should list this number in the notes field.

- **PURCHASE PRICE**

OPTIONAL ITEMS might include:

- **WHO YOU PURCHASED THE COIN FROM**
  This is a helpful reference for pedigree, recovery issues; particularly valuable if from a recognized auction house and sale. Often, your heirs will not know your major (trusted) sources of coins.

- **RELATED EXPENSES THAT WOULD IMPACT THE ACQUISITION COST**
  Acquisition expenses are part of the basis of your collection for estate purposes. If you traveled to an auction or coin convention to purchase coins, reasonable travel expenses relative to the amount purchased may be assigned (more on this later).

- **AN ISSUE NUMBERING SYSTEM**
  One easy method for sorting and organizing collection records by computer is the use of an issue numbering system that sequences each coin by denomination, date and mint mark. The Professional Coin Grading Service (PCGS) employs such a numbering system. Their numbers are widely recognized in the industry and can be found by acquiring a population report. An additional benefit in recording purchases using this system is that each PCGS coin has their issue identification number on the grading label.

- **AN INVENTORY NUMBERING SYSTEM**
  You might also benefit from having your own inventory numbering system to link the coins to the record. Numbers could be sequential (e.g. 00001), reflect the purchase date (e.g. 9912001), or any other

system that makes it easy to pick up a piece of your collection and quickly identify it in the record.

- **LOCATION**
  This is particularly important if your collection is extensive and spread out around your house, in safe-deposit boxes, in different banks, or other storage sites. Also, if you have annotated a group of coins as a single line item on your inventory, try to keep the coins together in one location.

CONTINUING ITEMS – Once your files are created, two ongoing functions are quite important to the process. One is annotating any items that you have sold or traded (can you imagine the amount of time your heirs would spend looking for listed coins if you neglected to note that you had sold them ten years prior?). The second is to create a periodic value update. The packaged software provides this option, but if you're creating your own file, you'll need to consider:

- **VALUE**

- **VALUE SOURCE**
  (e.g. "Red Book", Trends, Coin Dealer Newsletter) We would recommend that you use a wholesale pricing guide, as something approximating liquidation value is usually more beneficial for estate purposes. You should note the source, so your heirs can use the same one.

- **LAST EVALUATION DATE**
  We recommend that you update your records at least semi-annually and more frequently if you acquire and/or dispose of significant numbers of coins. Always date the evaluation on the inventory.

- **SALES DATE** (If Applicable)
  If you sell or trade something, please annotate it in your record. One way of addressing this is to conduct an annual inventory and note either that you found the coin or explain its absence.

Creating and maintaining the inventory record is paramount, but there are several related tasks that are also important.

- **RETAIN ALL PURCHASE INVOICES**

  The IRS loves receipts. Having the majority of your cost basis documented lends credibility to those entries for which no invoice was provided. We recommend that you file your invoices sequentially by purchase date and if you have created your own inventory-numbering system, mark the matching numbers on the invoice.

- **RETAIN RECEIPTS FOR RELATED EXPENSES**

  Certain expenses surrounding the acquisition, development and disposition of your collection may raise your cost basis, while others may be deductible in the current tax year. Grading service fees, shipping expenses, travel expenses and sales commissions or fees are examples. Rules vary too widely for any simple guideline beyond: keep every receipt and discuss your personal situation with your tax advisor.

- **MAINTAIN DUPLICATE RECORDS**

  Or back up your computer files. We recommend you keep one inventory at your primary place of residence and one off-site, perhaps in your safe deposit box with your other important papers. This is a safeguard against everything from your computer crashing to theft or natural disaster, and is valuable from both an estate planning and insurance claim standpoint.

- **RECORD YOUR WISHES IN WRITING**

  If you wish to leave your coin collection to a specific heir, or if you wish a specific coin or coins to go to different heirs, this MUST be in your will for it to be effective. New, separate lists should be provided to identify the division of your collection. A very good means of handling it is for you to physically segregate the coins, invoices and other records in accordance with your bequest. Alternatively, the general inventory can be annotated to identify the heir for each line item.

- **PLAYING "CATCH UP."**

  "What if I don't have the records and I've been collecting for many years? How can I recreate them and what is this 'basis' you're talking about?" Records are extremely important because in their absence, your basis for taxes (which basically means your cost) is the face value of the coins! The task of playing catch up is ponderous, but necessary to avoid an unnecessary tax bill. The IRS will generally accept recreated records that attest to the approximate time of purchase with contemporaneous values. The downside is that you will have to acquire the pricing guides for those periods and then maintain copies with your inventory.

In summary, the small steps you take each day in building a record along with your collection will create a valuable legacy. Good records will allow either an orderly disposition in your lifetime or will lessen the burden on your heirs at a time when they would much rather concentrate on honoring your memory. The alternative... well, that's discussed below and throughout the book, but it will involve an expensive and time-consuming effort on someone's part, at a time when they will least wish to do so.

TIPS FOR HEIRS OK, you've inherited a coin collection (or are attempting to evaluate one for probate) and the deceased maintained inadequate records or no records at all. What do you do to protect everyone's interests?

The first thing any professional you call is going to ask is whether you have an inventory list of the collection. It's imperative that you make one. If the deceased was a collector, even if there were no records, the coins are probably either in individual holders that identify the issue and (possibly) grade, or in albums that identify the issue. If not and the coins are all loose, you will need to identify the issue. We recommend that you acquire "A Guidebook of United States Coins," which should be available at your public library or may be purchased from a local bookstore for around $10.00. Better known as the "Redbook" for its cover color, this guide will identify each issue of U.S. coinage, show where the mint marks are located and list significant varieties. The "Redbook" also provides retail values, but as it is published annually, the prices given are often poor estimates.

Order your list from the smallest denomination and in date order within the denomination; then work forward. If the holder has a grade on it, include it. If any coins are certified, include the name of the certification service. If you are dealing with sets and partial sets, use your judgment in deciding what to list individually. If the "Redbook" indicates little value, you need not write down 75 different dates and mintmarks. For example, the "pennyboard" set of Lincoln Cents beginning in 1940 is only worth a few dollars complete and should be listed as one item. On the other hand, you do need to identify the more valuable coins in a set or partial set. If you have the 1909 – 1939 Lincoln Cents book and it contains only some of the coins, list it as a partial set and mention any issues that the guidebook shows as having a premium (e.g. "A partial Lincoln Cent set 1909 –1939, includes 1909-S, 1914-D, 1924-D and 1931-S").

When you have completed the list, you are ready for the next step. Appraisals are discussed in depth in their own chapter, but the key point here is that the list you create will assist the professionals you contact in determining the scope of your collection and the type of appraisal that will be most beneficial.

CHAPTER 2 – CARING FOR YOUR COLLECTION

"An ounce of prevention is worth a pound of cure...
and a LOT of money!"

State of preservation is one of two main factors influencing the value of a coin. Unfortunately, if you are unaware of proper storage and handling techniques, a coin's state of preservation can diminish while in your care. As a serious collector, you may already have a good understanding of the process, but it can be more complicated than it appears. Many products routinely sold and used by the numismatic community are potentially hazardous, and what may be acceptable as a short-term solution can damage your coins in the long run. Certainly, you'll want to take the long view, both for your continued collecting enjoyment and for the benefit of your heirs.

ENSURE THE PROPER STORAGE OF YOUR COINS

You probably view your collection from two perspectives: as items purchased for your personal enjoyment, but necessarily also, as a significant asset that must be considered and protected. No one rule applies for proper coin storage, as you will want to weigh the benefit of easy access versus the potential for loss. You will have to make a decision you feel comfortable with, but for general guidance, we recommend that the higher the grade and the more the value "spread" between adjacent grades, the more permanent the storage solution. For example, if you purchase or inherit an MS-65 coin worth $2,000 and the

MS-64 value is $500, the fiscal risk of inadvertent mishandling should far outweigh the desire for direct access.

OPTIONS FOR STORING INDIVIDUAL COINS AND CURRENCY

SEALED INERT CAPSULES – The most permanent solution for storing high-grade, valuable coins is to have them graded and encapsulated by one of the independent, third-party grading services. The methods and relative merits of this process are discussed further in Chapter 7 titled "Third-Party Authentication and Grading," but to summarize their storage role, each of the major grading services carefully places the coin in an inert plastic insert. This in turn is placed between two clear, hard plastic shells and ultrasonically sealed. When completed, the coins are virtually impervious to any accidental external damage, which makes the capsules, also routinely referred to as "slabs," the ideal choice for protecting important pieces. Warranties vary among the grading services. You should check with them for any specific questions.

The second tier of individual storage involves a wide selection of inert plastic holders that are not sonically sealed. Some examples include:

- Capitol Plastics™ holders
  Employ two pieces of clear, hard plexi-glass and a center piece of tinted plastic with a denominational aperture, held together with plastic screws. **NOTE** - These holders are fine for coins, but the similar, two-piece holder for currency compresses the bill and can make it lose its natural "waviness." Currency specialists recommend using only the chemically inert Mylar™ currency holders for your paper money.

- Kointains™
  Employ two round, form-fitting capsules that snap together around the coin and the finished product is then usually inserted into another container.

- Air-Tite™ holders
  Employ a foam aperture ring inside two snap-together round capsules. The completed capsule is then inserted in a square cardboard frame.

- Snap-Locs™
  Employ two pieces of square, molded hard plastic that have a frosted appearance except for the clear, denomination specific viewing windows. As the name implies, these two pieces snap together once the coin is placed on the bottom piece.

These holders are made of inert materials and offer decent protection for your coins. You should, however, be very careful when inserting and removing the coins from the holders, and in ensuring a snug fit with no "play." Because of their quality, these holders are somewhat expensive relative to the third tier, and some collectors are reluctant to use them unless the coin has a higher value level. That's reasonable, but it's also relative. You can look at the holder as a one-time insurance premium and determine from there what value warrants the usage of a "premium" holder.

The third tier represents the holders used for the vast majority of coins because of their relative affordability; it is in this tier that most problems occur. This is not to pan any particular product, but at this price level, each has its purpose and its limitations.

- 2 x 2 inch cardboard holders
  These stapled holders have been used by generations of collectors; they are a very popular and inexpensive way to house lower grade and low value coins. These consist of a 2 x 4 inch piece of card board that is lined with inert Mylar™ and has two cutouts slightly bigger than the coin being housed. The cardboard is folded in half with the coin inserted, and then stapled. Once folded, the holder attains the dimensions by which it is commonly known: "2 by 2." The longevity of this product is testimony to its usefulness, but there are limitations. The Mylar™ sheets in 2 x 2s are very thin and easily broken, particularly over time. When this occurs, outside contaminants can gain access to the coin. Cardboard contains sulfur, and when the Mylar™ is breached, toning from the holder itself can occur, but usually only at the point of the breach. Similarly, if the staples used are exposed to moisture and begin to rust, the rust can eventually reach and interact with the coin. The greatest danger from staples, however, is the accidental scratching of coins while removing them from the holder or damage to adjacent holders from unflattened staples. This is simply a matter

of patience. Always flatten all the staples after sealing a 2 x 2. Reversing the process, first totally remove all the staples before attempting to remove the coin.

- Vinyl "Flips"
These are now possibly the most popular method of housing single coins. These are two-pocket soft plastic holders with the coin going in one side and (usually) a card with relevant information inserted in the other. It is then folded in half ("flipped") so that the coin is in front of the card and the information and price can be read through the transparent plastic. Their popularity is due to the ease with which the coins can be removed and the information card updated. Vinyl flips can be a good short-term storage solution, but the very characteristics that make them so pliable present a long-term hazard. Soft flips are made with polyvinyl chloride, more commonly referred to as "PVC." In this application, the PVC is made pliable by the inclusion of an oil-based plasticizer or softening agent. Over time, this agent will leach out of the holder and onto the coin's surface. There, it may react with the alloy and eat into the coin's surface. Exposure to heat and moisture accelerates the process, so the danger is exacerbated in warm, humid areas. NOTE: It is the plasticizer that gets on the coin and creates the damage, not the PVC. Nonetheless, most collectors and dealers refer to the condition as PVC damage, or colloquially as "green slime." If you inspect your coins and see a green, oily film on them, you will need to take immediate action to reverse the process (methods are explained later in this chapter).

- Mylar™ "Hard Flips"
Hard flips are the polar opposites of the soft flip. They contain no plasticizer and present no chemical danger to the coins. Unfortunately, this is accomplished at the price of being very brittle, and over time, they become more likely to crack. Insertion and removal of coins is more difficult and hard edges require more care during handling. Risk is increased if the Mylar™ cracks and leaves sharp edges.

- Polyethylene Bags
A popular short-term solution employed by the grading services is this combination of a polyethylene bag and a soft flip. The polyethylene bag is both chemically inert and soft, hence coins are easily inserted and removed. The limitation is that polyethylene is not transparent and the coins must be removed to be inspected. A lesser-known fact is that polyethylene does breathe, so while it would impede the transfer of plasticizer from a PVC flip to the coin, it may not stop it if enough time elapses. Backing up a step, a good rule of thumb is that soft flips are NEVER a long-term storage solution, regardless of what is used with them.

- 2 x 2 Paper Envelopes
This is another inexpensive option that has been around for decades...long enough to demonstrate its main limitation. Paper envelopes contain sulfur, which is highly reactive with metals. Occasionally, long term usage results in very pretty toning, but more often, the result is a thick, dull-gray patina that is firmly ingrained in the coin's surface. This toning is not attractive, will not easily dip off, and usually severely diminishes the original mint luster in either case, thus reducing the coin's value. As such, we recommend that if you must use paper envelopes, please insert the coin in a Kointain™ or "poly bag" first.

- Mylar™ Currency Holders
These are our only recommended holder for paper money. Chemically inert, the holders are both stiff enough to protect the note and flexible enough to preserve its natural texture. The one caveat: when inserting the note into the holder, special care should be taken to avoid bending corners, an act which could have a serious, negative financial impact on the value of the note.

OPTIONS FOR STORING "GROUPS" OF COINS AND CURRENCY

Options for storing groups of coins and currency are widely varied as to style and cost depending on the value and type of material, and the display requirements of the owner. As with the individual holders, the possible problems are not always obvious and usually come when the holder is used in a manner or role for which it was not intended.

- Rolls & Tubes
  Uncirculated coins that were machine-wrapped in paper rolls are highly prized by numismatists for their originality and the potential for high-grade examples. Usually, the two coins at the ends become toned from the sulfur in the paper, but this is accepted as further "proof" of their originality. Bank wrapped rolls should generally be left intact for this reason. Other paper tubes tend to break down over time and spill their contents at the most inconvenient moment. Commercially sold tubes are available in both hard and soft plastic. Both are suitable for long-term storage with the caveat that the hard plastic becomes more brittle with age. The soft tubes are made of PVC, but we have seen no evidence to date that they contain the plasticizer that plagues the flips.

- Books and Binders for sets
  As with the individual holders, you can buy a wide variety of holders for coin sets at various price levels. The most basic is the "penny board." Coins are pushed into slightly smaller holes in the cardboard page and held by perimeter pressure. This is only suitable for circulated coins, as the pushing process itself could put thumbprints on higher-grade material and the holder offers no protection from further contact. Most people recognize this, however. The main problems occur with more expensive albums, where the perceived safety is greater than the reality.

The next tier features coin albums with sliding plastic strips that provide windows for a row or rows of coins. These albums are considerably more expensive than the penny boards and too often, people assume that they are 100% safe. There are, in fact, two culprits to beware of:

- The plastic strips in older albums of this type were often made with plasticizer-softened PVC with all those inherent problems.

- The second generation of strips is made from inert, hard plastic. That in itself does not cause problems, but moving the strips back and forth to insert or remove coins can! If an uncirculated or proof coin is not inserted fully into its slot (and sometimes this cannot be done at all), the sliding hard plastic can abrade the high points of the coin's surface and effect a significant reduction in value in the process!

Another solution for sets is the Lucite™ holder or board. Lucite is chemically inert and the boards are held together with plastic screws. These holders provide good visibility and protection from external threat. Their limitation is that sometimes the apertures are slightly too large for specific coins, which then rotate, or worse, bang around in their slot. Some people attempt to cure this with various "shims," but in doing so, risk a chemical reaction with the shim material. If you are faced with this condition, please be careful to pick an inert material to hold the coin in place. Also, many screws must be handled for each coin inserted.

- Currency Options
  As with the individual holders, currency should not be stored in a Lucite™ holder where the paper is compressed. Neither should it be put into PVC plastic pages without first being inserted in the recommended Mylar™ individual holder. There are some commercially available "book shelf" albums available for currency. You would need to ascertain that the "windows" are chemically inert and that the physical design does not compress the note. Relatively speaking, there are fewer commercial group options for storing a currency collection and collectors have become quite innovative in finding solutions. One of the best we've seen is an expandable, manila check portfolio that should be available in any office supply store and many department stores.

- Other Storage Options
  Large quantities of coins are usually transported in canvas bags from the Mint to banks. There they are counted and broken down into rolls as needed. Typically, numismatists use this method as well for bulk storage and transport. Canvas can make sense, but here are the caveats:

  1. Canvas contains sulfur. The rainbow "crescent" toning often seen on silver dollars is from the chemical reaction of the coin surface that was in contact with the bag. In this instance, the result is good; in others…maybe not.

2. The state of preservation of uncirculated coins diminishes each time they're transported loose in a bag. In the best of circumstances, the coins shift and rub against each other. In the worst (like mint employees throwing bags around), surface abrasions to some coins may be severe: hence the term, "bag marks."

We recommend that you use canvas bags only for circulated coins or for bulk mint state pieces where individual grade is not a factor. The sole exception would be if you have a "mint sewn" bag of uncirculated coins. In this case, this increases the value perception by potential buyers because they know the bag has not been "picked over." If you have a mint sewn bag, handle it with care, but leave it intact until you are ready to show the contents to every potential buyer.

- "ORIGINAL ISSUE" HOLDERS
  Proof sets, mint sets and many commemoratives come from the Mint prepackaged in issue-specific holders. In the vast majority of cases, coins should be left in their original packing because the lack of it often leads to discounting and some of the holders have value in their own rights.

STORAGE LOCATIONS

Physical security will be discussed in the next chapter, but where you keep your coins also impacts their state of preservation. Ideally, coins should be stored in an environment of consistent moderate temperature and low humidity. A bank safe deposit box fits these criteria, as does an air-conditioned home. These are not, however, always a given.

If you live in Arizona, the humidity is low and you probably have air-conditioning. In Michigan, this may not be the case and you have wild swings in temperature extremes between the seasons. Collectors in South Florida battle high humidity and salt air. It would seem obvious that regardless of where you live, coins should be stored indoors. Nonetheless, we have seen collections stored in garages, outdoor storage units and occasionally buried in the ground! Storing your collection in an environment with a controlled climate is one of the first steps you can take to preserve its value.

Moisture and humidity are culprits that can seriously damage coins. You probably learned early in school what happens when water and metal are in contact for long periods of time. Copper is a particularly reactive metal and is used as an alloy in most United States coins. Corrosion and spotting often result when coins are exposed to moisture or humidity. Bags of silica gel can be used to retard humidity but need to be replaced regularly. The best solution is to simply find a low-humidity environment for your coins, even if it means the inconvenience of a safe-deposit box.

Currency has its own special requirements, but when properly housed, is more durable than one might believe. High humidity should be avoided, but currency should receive some air to maintain its natural fiber. The main culprit for notes is too much direct sunlight, as overexposure will cause the ink to fade and diminish the value. Otherwise, normally cautious packing and storage should be sufficient.

RESTORING YOUR COLLECTION

You should inspect your collection every six months to make sure your coins are not being exposed to potential hazards. If you find a problem, or if the information provided in this chapter reveals a potential problem you had been unaware of, how do you correct it? Damage to coins is either mechanical or chemical. If the threat is mechanical, simply change the coins to a location or holder that does not present the threat. If the threat is chemical, you first need to determine the immediacy of the danger.

Soft flips are usually OK for the short-term, and if you've just started using them, you may need only to make a plan for alternative long-term storage. If however, you can see a film on the surface of the coins, they need to be removed immediately from the offending holders and transferred to inert holders. This would prove futile, of course, unless the plasticizer is first removed from the coins.

Ironically, more coins have been damaged with good intentions than with bad ones. As such, we mention cleaning options with great trepidation. Unless you are prepared to carefully learn the techniques and practice them with great patience, you would really be better off paying a professional to do the job for you. In either case, no matter how much care is taken, you must also be prepared to accept some cases where the result does not meet your expectations!

- Removing PVC Plasticizer

The plasticizer is oily and cannot be removed simply by washing with water. A solvent is the key and the simplest solution is acetone. This can be purchased commercially, or for small jobs, a bottle of "non-oily" nail polish remover is primarily acetone.

1. If possible, acquire a pair of plastic tongs.

2. Do the work near a running water source.

3. Put the acetone in one small dish and some rubbing alcohol in a second dish.

4. Dip and swirl the coin in the acetone for several seconds, then rinse with hot water.

5. Carefully examine the coin's surface to see if the "oily" look has disappeared. If not, repeat the process.

6. When the plasticizer has been removed, dip the coin in the alcohol to neutralize the surface and blot the coin dry (DO NOT RUB) with paper towels.

7. Protect the coin in an inert holder.

NOTE 1 – Do not attempt this process with copper coins. Copper is highly reactive and acetone may change its color, thus diminishing the value substantially. If you discover PVC on a copper coin, take it to a professional, but even then, understand that the odds of restoring it to full originality are far from guaranteed.

NOTE 2 – If the plasticizer resists your attempts at removal and you lose patience, please take the coins to a professional. Taking more drastic measures on your own will likely have an undesired result!

NOTE 3 – You are REALLY better off letting professionals do this!

In summary, caring for your collection is an ongoing process that requires product knowledge, careful planning and routine maintenance. If you've been taking your collection for granted, it's due for an inspection now!

TIPS FOR HEIRS If you are not a coin collector, you can do your inheritance more harm than good by almost any attempt to "improve" the collection.

If you did not receive good records and/or guidance in the estate and need to go through the inventory process explained in Chapter 1, the following three rules are basic, yet extremely important:

- Coins should always be held between the thumb and index finger touching only the edge of the coin. Never directly touch the front surface of the coin (known as the obverse) or the back surface (known as the reverse). Natural oils in your skin and/or other contaminants on your fingers leave behind fingerprints that can severely affect a coin's salability and value. Copper and nickel are particularly reactive and susceptible to fingerprints. In short, you should only touch coins the minimum needed to identify the date, mint mark and variety, and it is preferable to accomplish that with out touching them at all.

- **DO NOT attempt to clean any of the coins.** The very "dirt" or "tarnish" that is perceived negatively by a non-collector is often prized by the collector for its originality. There are exceptions, but you should consult with a professional to determine what they are. The professional should also give you free advice on storage options and which holders are best for your coins.

- This rule also applies to currency. It's not unusual for older currency to have pencilled notations on its surfaces. As some are tempted to clean the "dirty" coin, so are others inclined to erase the offending writing. Please DO NOT attempt to do this. The writing will more than likely NOT come off and the attempt will be both damaging and irrevocable! If you have old currency that was in a box or between the pages of a book, get some Mylar™ holders from a local dealer and store the notes in them. If you have currency in old holders that look "oily," take them to a professional for advice rather than trying to improve them.

If you did receive good records and/or guidance and wish to dispose of the collection, you should deliver the coins or currency to the prospective buyer or auction house "as is" and discuss care issues if the professionals say they have significance. If you are keeping the collection, you may still wish to have a professional examine it to determine if any care problems exist. This is money well spent and it is highly encouraged.

CHAPTER 3 – SAFEGUARDING YOUR COLLECTION

"Do you want your collection... more than the thief does?"

The sad truth is that crimes against property are on the rise. Burglary and simple theft almost qualify as growth businesses. The current arrest and conviction rate is abysmal, and restoration of property even worse! Some of our employees were recently victims of an airport "snatch and grab." The good news was that what the thieves thought were coin cases held only supplies. The bad news was that despite being provided both perpetrator descriptions and a license plate number, the police were not optimistic... or perhaps more accurately, not interested. The fact that the thieves got the wrong bags made the case relatively "insignificant" in the overall scope of things! We don't know if that kind of attitude is endemic; perhaps there are only enough personnel resources to handle the more serious crimes these days. In any event, it certainly illustrates the need for each of us to upgrade our own attitudes concerning security, particularly if we own the kind of valuables prized by thieves... like a coin collection.

SECURITY VERSUS ACCESS –
A Timeless Quandary

Most collectors like to have their coins close at hand so that they can study them at their leisure. In a nutshell, that's what collecting is all about. The prospect of routinely transporting the collection to and from a safe-deposit box is tiresome at best. Conversely, no one wants to lose his or her favorite coins to a burglar. The unfortunate thing is that the inconvenience is constant and the significance of security is only drilled home after you've been robbed. As a result, even people who know better may become lax over time. To avoid this, write your own personal security plan and include these elements:

- Home Security – your coin collection is at risk from theft, fire, water damage and other natural disasters. If you are going to keep substantial value at your residence, you should employ several proactive measures to protect them.

  1. Monitored Security System
  A security system is the core of any security plan. Includes both theft and fire alarms that are monitored externally and reported immediately to police and fire departments if triggered. Hardware can be installed for a few hundred to a few thousand dollars and monitoring is only a nominal monthly expense, currently around $25-$75. A monitored security system sends most burglars looking for easier game and puts the more daring ones on the clock. Once the system perimeter is breached, the burglar has only the response time to grab what he can and attempt an escape. The following devices and practices are designed to minimize what a burglar can locate in a hurry.

  2. Home Safe
  Safes offer obvious deterrent value against theft, but have additional value in the event of fire or natural disaster. Costs are based on size and fire (temperature) "TL" rating and you should make your choice only after discussing your particular needs with an expert. Many insurance companies require a home safe to write a collectibles rider to your Homeowner's Policy while others will discount the rider based on the quantity and quality of the safeguards you employ.

  3. Deterrent Practices
  Whether or not you employ a security system or a safe, there are things you can do to reduce the risk of a successful burglary. Primary is to always leave the impression that someone is at home. This can be accomplished in part by remembering to have your paper and mail held while you're

out of town and by putting one or more of your lights on timers. "Beware of Dog" signs (whether or not you own one) on the back fence may well send the prospective burglar on to a petless victim.

4. Valuables Camouflage
Most people are predictable, and burglars know all the "good" hiding places. They do, however, still have those external or self-imposed time constraints to contend with. The longer a burglar stays in a house, the greater the likelihood of capture and the burglars know that, too! Things you should know and avoid – most people keep their valuables in the master bedroom followed closely by their home offices if they have one. Guess where burglars go first? Leave decoys. One gentleman we know has numerous coin albums in plain sight on the bookshelves… filled with pocket change. Another acquaintance has an old safe that is heavy but moveable. It sits in the corner of his home office and contains absolutely nothing! Its predecessor was taken in a burglary where the thief left several thousand dollars worth of electronic and musical equipment because he thought he'd hit the jackpot. The acquaintance now has a monitored security system and modern (wall) safe, but keeps the decoy as a reminder of the importance of security, and perhaps just a bit of humor about the burglar who only got an empty box (and maybe a hernia). If you don't have a safe, small valuables are best hidden in a false outlet with something plugged into it. A coin collection should be spread over several non-obvious locations. While you may not be able to totally foil a burglar, you may at least be able to minimize his success.

- Off-Site Storage & Transport
The primary off-site storage option is a safe-deposit box either at a bank or private vault. If you can find a location close to either home or work, the inconvenience factor can be minimized. Sites with weekend access are a major plus, but they are scarce. There's no question that safe-deposit boxes offer very secure storage, but don't let that lull you into complacency. There are still a few storage and security guidelines you need to remember and follow.

1. Rent a box that's big enough to hold everything comfortably.

2. Use a desiccant such as silica gel to remove any moisture, and change it regularly.

3. Never forget that your greatest security danger is in transporting the coins to and from the box. Use a nondescript bag or carry-all to hold the coins, and try not to carry too much weight at one time.

4. Have someone drive you to the box site or park as close to the entrance as possible to minimize your time on the street with the coins.

5. Avoid establishing a pattern in picking up or dropping off your coins.

6. Be aware of what's happening around you when transporting your coins. Check your rearview mirror frequently. If you think a vehicle may be following you, do not drive directly to your home. Make several detours that do not follow any logical traffic pattern and see if you lose the suspect vehicle. Know where the closest police station is and if you become firmly convinced that you are being followed, drive directly there.

7. Carry a cell phone with you when transporting coins. A frightening new robbery technique is to rear-end a vehicle and then rob the victim when they get out to assess the damage and exchange insurance information. You'll have to use your judgment for the situation, but if you're carrying coins and get rear-ended, you should stay in the car and call 911 on the cell phone. Don't hesitate to tell the operator that you're carrying valuables and are concerned about the possibility of robbery. If you really believe that it's a setup, don't stop; call 911 and tell them your intent while driving to the police station.

8. Airports have also become a favorite work place for thieves. There's a steady flow of people, noise, confusion and a sense of urgency from trying to meet deadlines in an unfamiliar environment. The usual method is the snatch and grab; the thief targets someone who appears distracted, grabs their briefcase or bag and melts into the crowd. A variation is to work in teams where baggage is being unloaded at the curb. One or more of the thieves will distract the victim, while others will grab the bags and then all will make their escape in a waiting vehicle. Your only protection is constant vigilance. You should always have either a grip or your foot on any case containing valuables and should become doubly suspicious if a stranger tries to engage you in conversation. Strange as it sounds, some people carry a loud whistle when transporting valuables. If someone attempts to grab a bag and you start blowing the whistle, the thief loses control of the situation and is put on the defensive. Everyone else in the area stops to see what the noise is all about so the thief loses the camouflage of the crowd.

- Shipping
  Occasionally, you may need to ship coins to another party, and again, there are rules to follow that will minimize the possibility of loss. First and foremost, do not put anything on the outside of the package that would hint at its contents. If an address contains identifying words - coins, numismatics, or anything similar - use initials instead! Additionally, look at the container you're using. We recently received a package from another dealer whose mailing address labels used initials, but the shipping person packed the coins in a "Redbook" box that was clearly marked, "Guidebook of U.S. Coins."

Pack the coins securely so that they do not rattle and betray their presence. Loose space in tubes should be filled. Pieces of styrofoam "peanuts" are good for this purpose. Make sure that your shipping box is strong enough for the included weight and bind it with strapping tape. If you are using Registered Mail (the preferred method for most collectors), the post office has a requirement that all access seams be sealed with an approved paper tape.

Method of shipment is a choice that weighs value, risk and cost. USPS 1st Class or Priority Mail with Insurance is the most cost-effective method up to $500 value. The rate of loss has dropped considerably over the last decade, so this is a reasonable option for inexpensive items that can be replaced. Above $500 value, Registered Mail with Postal Insurance is both cost-effective and extremely safe. The one caveat is that the real insurance maximum for registered mail is $25,000. The Post Office wants you to indicate if the contents exceed that amount, and will charge you more for a higher claimed value; they will not, however, pay more than $25,000 on a claim. If you have more value than that, you will need to send multiple packages or seek supplemental private insurance. FEDEX, UPS and other private shippers have become popular in recent years. They offer fast, guaranteed delivery with a high success rate. They also appear to offer some insurance options, but rare coins are specifically excluded! You will need to get private insurance coverage if you wish to use one of these shippers, or you may ask the other party if they have a shipper account and insurance that would cover the shipment.

- Insurance
  No matter how many security measures you employ to protect your collection, you also need to acquire suitable insurance to protect you should you suffer a loss of part or all of the collection. This can also be a complicated area as insurance companies write policies in a language all their own. We're not trying to pan insurance companies; they're in business to make money and they perform a valuable service. As someone seeking protection, though, you need to understand that contract language will generally favor the insurance company, and you need to know exactly what you're getting. That means asking questions. In the case of coins, you particularly need to be sure what coverages apply when the coins are at home, in a safe-deposit box or in transit, as well as any additional security requirements for each circumstance. It is not a cut-and-dried situation. For example:

1. Most Home Owner's policies DO NOT insure your coin collection beyond $1,000 (combined with everything else defined as a "valuable"). Your insurance company can usually offer you a rider for more specific coverage, but as it's not their regular business, they're usually not very flexible. You would have to provide a fixed inventory and it would likely be a major paperwork exercise to change it when you buy or sell.

2. Some insurance companies may require an "appraisal for insurance." If you choose a company that has this requirement, guidance is available in Chapter 8, covering appraisals.

3. Like most business circumstances, you should analyze your options against your personal situation and then shop for the best deal. In this specialized field, the best option often comes from a company that is familiar with the needs of coin collectors. If this route appeals to you, we have listed several companies in the Appendix titled, "Insurance Companies Offering Numismatic Coverage."

Coins are popular with burglars and thieves. Regretfully, the risk involved means you need to temper your enjoyment of collecting with some caution. In addition to the measures already suggested, you need to be careful with who knows that you collect coins, and more particularly, where you keep them. It's said that any piece of information shared with one person reaches ten, and an interesting piece of information... well, use your imagination. Enjoy your collection, but stay vigilant!

TIPS FOR HEIRS This chapter contains information that may be the most important you will read. Seasoned coin collectors are generally very security conscious, but those who only recently have come into possession of a collection must immediately understand the risks and responsibilities that come with this unfamiliar asset. Most importantly, get the collection to a safe deposit box immediately. Until you have it safely tucked into a bank vault, don't tell *anyone* about your collection.

PART 2
ESTATE PLANNING FOR YOUR COLLECTION

CHAPTER 4 - INCLUDE YOUR FAMILY IN YOUR PLANS

"Planning for your eventual passing is unpleasant at best,
but the best time to start planning for it is today."

We seriously doubt any adult in America has not read or heard of the importance of making a will, and yet every year, tens of thousands of Americans who would have benefited from wills die intestate. The reason is simple: nobody likes to think about death, much less actively prepare for it. It may be even worse for collectors. As much as people hate to contemplate their own demise, collectors are equally loath to consider the sale of their coins. Perhaps they equate the two events.

Since you're reading this book, we hope that you are at least willing to think about the ultimate disposition of your coins. Whether you intend to collect to the end, or sell next month, much of the same advice applies. We have helped more than 15,000 people dispose of their collections, and more than 20% were heirs who knew next to nothing about rare coins. That is a statistic that we would like to change – you should too!

Involve Your Family

Many collectors keep their families in the dark about the scale and nature of their collecting. We understand that the reasons for this may be myriad and viewed strictly in the present sense, they may very well suit your situation and preference. Taking a longer view, however, have you considered what effect an untimely demise might have on your collection? What would your heirs' expectations be? We have seen both extremes.

One call from Widow Smith brought us to a house with the dining room table covered with boxes of world coins to a height of three feet. From a distance, it was one of the most impressive collections that we had ever inspected: all matching coin boxes, all neatly labeled with the countries of origin. The widow told us that her husband had been a serious collector for more than three decades, visiting his local coin shop very nearly every Saturday. He then came home and meticulously prepared his purchases, spending hour upon happy hour at the table in his little study. We opened the first box, and couldn't help but notice the neat and orderly presentation: cardboard 2x2s, neatly stapled, crisp printing of country name, year of issue, Yeoman number, date purchased, and amount paid. We also couldn't help but notice that 90% of the coins had been purchased for less than 50 cents, and the balance for less than one dollar. The collection was box after box of post-1940 minors, all impeccably presented… all essentially worthless.

We asked the Widow Smith if she had any idea of the value of the collection. She replied that she knew that rare coins were valuable, and since her late husband had worked so diligently on his collection for so many years, she hoped it would enable her to afford a nice retirement in Florida. It was obviously a very delicate moment. We had to very carefully explain that we were neither interested in the coins for auction, nor for direct purchase. Her husband had enjoyed himself thoroughly for all those years, but he had never told her that he was spending more on holders, staples and boxes than he was on the coins. Her dreams of comfortable retirement dashed, we put her in touch with two dealers who routinely purchase such coins (perhaps not surprisingly, she refused to consider an offer from the local dealer who had sold most of these coins to her husband). Mr. Smith's fault was not in his collecting, for his love of these coins was manifest, but in his failure to let his wife know exactly what he was doing.

We more typically encounter widows and heirs on the other extreme. When your spouse spends $50,000 or $100,000 on rare coins, you generally have some knowledge of those purchases… but not always, and not always to the full extent of the purchases. Rare coins at this level are definitely an asset that needs to be given appropriate consideration. Unfortunately, however, because they are a hard asset, and one that easily falls outside of prying eyes, some heirs make their distributions without first gathering all of the facts.

Miss Jones was the younger of two sisters who were dividing their father's estate. Dad had left Germany in the early 1930s. As historians will note, this was not particularly a great time to emigrate to America, although it was certainly an excellent time to be leaving Germany. Dad brought to America two collections: antique silver service pieces and his rare coins. The coins were mostly sold to establish his mercantile concern in Iowa. He prospered despite the hard times, and he spent the next thirty years rebuilding his collection of Germanic/European coinage. At the same time, he kept expanding his collection of silverware lovingly created by 17th & 18th century German silversmiths. We knew every aspect of his collecting history, because he had left a meticulous record on index cards. Every coin, every piece of silver was detailed with his cataloging and purchase history. Even his own daughter was moved to compliment his passion for keeping such detailed records.

After his death, his daughters decided to split his collections outside of probate. They added up the purchase values of each of his collections. We do not think it was coincidental that the two collections came out just about equal. The older sister/executor had some small knowledge of antique silver, and since she wished to keep all of the elegant heirloom tea service for herself, she decided to keep the silver and give her younger sister the coins. She was definitely not interested in splitting the heirlooms. She sold the non-family silver pieces through a regional auction house, and bragged of realizing more than $200,000 from her father's $27,000 investment.

The younger sister came to us with just one box of his coins. Her father's records for that box indicated a cost less than $2,000, but knowing the years when he had collected, we were anticipating at least a few nice coins. We were, however, totally unprepared for the numismatic feast which was laid before us: pristine coins of the greatest rarity... wonderful, gorgeous coins, most of which had been off the market for at least twenty years! His "$2,000" box was worth more than $150,000, surpassing her wildest expectations.

Miss Jones then produced the record cards for the rest of the collection, and we offered to travel back to Iowa with her the same day. When we finished auctioning the coins, she had realized more than $1.2 million.

One more example of what can happen when information is not shared, and we warn you, the ending is a bit of a shocker! The wife of a deceased coin dealer once called us to consign one million dollars in rare coins from her late husband's estate. Since her self-employed husband had been ill for some time, this asset represented a significant portion of her entire retirement funding. We eagerly picked up the coins, and had already begun cataloging and photographing when we received an urgent phone call from her attorney. The coins had to be returned immediately! It seems that her husband had been holding the extensive coin purchases of his main customer in his vaults, and he had neither informed his wife nor adequately marked the boxes. Most of her $1 million retirement asset belonged to someone else! Failure to adequately inform heirs doesn't happen just to collectors!

A final example, one that really distressed us, demonstrates that partial planning, no matter how well intentioned, can't always guarantee the desired results. A collector with a sizeable collection divided his coins equally (by value) between his adult son and daughter, with instructions that they should seek expert advice before selling. The daughter came to us, and we were pleased to report that her father had done an excellent job of dividing the collection – frankly, as expertly as we could have advised. The daughter's coins were worth in excess of $85,000. After she signed the Consignment Agreement, she told us the rest of the story. Her brother had sold his share two months earlier to a local pawnbroker for less than $7,500. Her father hadn't shared his knowledge of the asset's value with his children for fear that his son would spend the money foolishly... instead, her brother gave it away!

So, what should you do to prevent these kinds of problems?

Get your family involved, one way or another!

One of the greatest joys of collecting involves not just the coins and currency, but the friends we make along the way. If passing your collection to the next generation is desirable, you will want to organize an orderly transition. If they just aren't interested in sharing your love of coins, you will have to decide whether to dispose of the collection in your lifetime, or pass that task to your heirs. If the latter, your family should – at a minimum – have a basic understanding of your collection, its approximate value, and how you want it dispersed.

Important Questions to Be Discussed

- Are there heirs who will want the collection from a collector's standpoint?

- Where are the coins kept?

- Where is the inventory of the coins kept?

- What is the approximate value of the collection?

- Do any of the coins in your possession belong to someone else?

- Is there a numismatist that you trust to provide guidance to your heirs?

- Is there a firm you and your heirs will wish to use to aid in the collection's disposition after your death?

In summary, talk with your family about your collection. The horror stories beginning this chapter are all true and they won't be the last. If for whatever reason, you cannot bring yourself to share this information with your whole family, pick one trusted individual… perhaps whomever you are considering to be your Executor. If even that won't work for you, please take the time to write detailed instructions, or simply make notes in this book, and leave it in your safe-deposit box or wherever you keep your coins. The next few chapters will further define your options and finding help to implement them. Whatever your choices, the written instructions can be either part of your will or at the very least, a document kept with the collection inventory. Your heirs will thank you for this final attention to details!

TIPS FOR HEIRS This chapter doesn't address inheritance issues, but communications can be initiated from any direction. Do you have a parent with a collection? Certainly it is an issue that requires tact, but such a discussion may save considerable heartache and misfortune later. Additionally, if you know in advance that your spouse or relative has named you as Executor in a will, a few conversations about the collection will make your job much easier.

CHAPTER 5 – DIVISION OF ASSETS

"No single event has greater potential for dividing a family than dividing an inheritance."

Inheritances bring out the best in some people and the worst in others. It's a sad fact that within even the most stable families, some members will view their relative worth only in tangible terms. In the highly charged emotional environment surrounding the loss of a loved one, any weaknesses in the relationships of those left behind are magnified. Suspicious minds are a bit more finely honed and if the estate is left to the survivors to divide, it doesn't take much of a spark to ignite a small conflagration! You can minimize the likelihood of a family melt-down by seeking sound legal advice in preparing your will and by leaving precise, written instructions dividing your assets among your heirs.

Instructions in regard to coin collections are particularly important because they generally involve a large number of pieces with valuations that are not obvious based on the coins' "looks." That can cause the perception of value to be nebulous and therefore, potentially contentious.

The simplest option (administratively) is to leave the collection intact to one heir. You should have the collection appraised (see Chapter 8 titled "Getting Your Collection Appraised) and may at your option, use that basis in dividing the balance of your estate. If your estate contains other collections besides coins (and an equal or structured division is part of your plan), you should have the other collections appraised as well to determine parity. Your attorney can provide the appropriate verbiage for your will. This is stated as the simplest option because there is no question as to the physical division of the collection after your death.

If you split the coin collection among your heirs, the paperwork burden increases. You must then detail what individual pieces go to whom, expand the scope of the appraisal, and more precisely define the locations of each recipient's portion. Alternatively, you may decree "equal shares." This will also require a detailed appraisal, but may create problems if two heirs want the same coins, or if some heirs want coins and others want to sell. You should objectively consider your family dynamics in making this decision.

We frequently hear the lament that nobody else in the family cares about coins. Perhaps it's because so many numismatists get serious with their collecting after their kids are grown. We know how difficult it can be to budget for coins when there are dentist bills, clothing, food and tuition bills to pay. By the time the kids are grown, most of them have developed their own hobbies and interests. Be that as it may, we doubt that you would want your family to suffer financially over their choice of leisure activities. A simpler alternative here is to make a will directing that the coins be sold, with the proceeds shared equally instead of the cumbersome process of dividing a collection equally.

The question arises whether the collection should be disposed of in your lifetime. From our experience with thousands of these situations, we can affirm that it is easier to divide the proceeds of a sale than the coins themselves. The reasons are quite logical. Members of your family may vicariously appreciate the pleasure that your collection brought to you, but unless they are coin collectors themselves, they are unlikely to keep your coins. If you can accept that, ask yourself whether they would handle the disposition as carefully and knowledgeably as you would? If this represents a significant asset to them, are they prepared to manage it properly?

We can understand if you are simply unable to part with your treasures, particularly if working with your collection is a major activity and source of enjoyment in your life at present. If this is the case, we strongly recommend that you prepare written disposition plan for your heirs and keep it with your inventory. Whether you intend to collect for three years, seven or a lifetime, you need to prepare now as if you may not be available to provide guidance later. These are hard words, but we doubt that any numismatist wants to see their family suffer a financial loss through the combination of poor planning and an untimely demise or incapacitation.

The upside of choosing disposition in your lifetime is that you retain control of the process and possibly garner some recognition of your collecting accomplishments. You also minimize the possibility of an uninformed disposition after your death. You might think that since it's harder to spend rare coins than cash, that such a gift will prevent idiotic behavior, but the pawnshop story mentioned previously is just one of many that we've heard.

Another option that bears mentioning is the gift of your collection to charity. Some collectors have substantial capital gains in their collections and a charitable gift makes a great deal of sense for their particular situations. If you entertain such thoughts, we must also point out that most charities know virtually nothing about coins or disposing of such assets. If you wish for your donation to make a lasting contribution, you will want to ensure that the charity receives the top dollar from your coins. In this case, unless you are donating the collection to a museum that will display it, it is probably better to sell in your lifetime while you can see the good works that the donation can create. You should talk with the charity and your lawyer or tax adviser to determine what specific option(s) would best suit your individual situation.

If you simply cannot bear the idea of selling your collection, then you must leave detailed instructions for the disposition of your gift. Most charities will have little real knowledge, and even less affection for your collection than a family heir. They would much rather spend their efforts putting your cash to good use than converting your collection to cash. (Conversely, we just sold a $50,000+ rarity for a Michigan charitable institution that was donated as a "common" coin. In all situations, professional knowledge is the key!) We recommend that your collection be sold via a numismatic auction, with the charity of your choice named as beneficiary. This solution ensures that you can keep your collection for your lifetime, that the collection will receive knowledgeable treatment in its disposition, and that your charity will receive the maximum return without expending its personnel resources. You can also recommend or designate a specific auctioneer to handle the disposition.

In summary, your collection is yours to enjoy now and yours to dispose of as you see fit. The old saw says, "You can't take it with you." You can, however, ensure that either the collection or its proceeds provide as much positive influence for others as it has for you.

- Make an action plan for your collection, even if you anticipate many more decades of collecting. You can always update it as you go… you cannot, however, start one once you're gone!

- Read the remaining chapters in this book for options.

- Talk with your advisors and determine which recipient(s), timing and method of disposition make the most sense for you.

- If the timing is now, select the agent appropriate to the method and proceed accordingly.

- If the timing is later, prepare detailed written instructions and leave copies with both your coins and your will. If you prefer your coins to be distributed among family members, leave specific instructions how that distribution is to be accomplished. If you prefer to distribute the proceeds, make sure you leave directions for non-numismatists to follow in contacting a firm that is trustworthy. Your instructions should be as detailed as necessary to accomplish your wishes.

TIPS FOR HEIRS This is another chapter which can aid you only if someone else reads and heeds it. You can, however, point it out to your loved one and discuss it with them whenever it seems politic. Good communications between family members often helps everyone avoid the pitfalls of estate planning and transfer. Maybe getting involved in Dad's coin collecting activities will create a new and lasting bond. You may even come to enjoy collecting yourself!

CHAPTER 6 – TAX OPTIONS FOR ESTATE PLANNING

"Taxes are usually underpaid out of intent,
but overpaid out of ignorance."

Once again, the United States tax code has run amok. Much as casino gambling rules are written to favor the house, so is the tax code written to favor the government. The core advantage is that the government's representatives can claim you owe virtually anything, and the burden of proving otherwise is on you! Throw in the continuing annual "improvements," Congressionally mandated exceptions, exemptions and "simplifications," and the result is well beyond the ken of most if not all Americans. Indeed, even IRS employees manning the tax help hotline give wrong advice roughly 20% of the time!

It is both ironic and symptomatic that the IRS does not accept financial responsibility for those errors. Similarly, while the IRS may recalculate a mathematical error in your favor, they will not point out legitimate deductions that would have reduced your tax bill. Nor will they advise you on how both your financial holdings and estate can be legally structured and positioned to minimize the tax bites of capital gains and estate taxes. That is your responsibility and right or wrong, is a reality you need to deal with… and if your holdings are substantial, well worth the expense of engaging experts to lead you through the fiscal minefield.

This chapter deals with some of the options available for estates with collections of coins and collectibles. Depending on your personal circumstances, the decisions you make may impact the amount of ordinary income, capital gains, gift and/or estate taxes that you or your heirs have to pay. The chapter is provided solely to improve your general understanding, for we cannot know or advise how any of the options would apply to your personal situation or holdings. We strongly recommend that after digesting this information, you engage the services of a competent legal professional, preferably an attorney who is board-certified in Real Estate, Trusts and Probate by your state, or a tax advisor, preferably a CPA who specializes in taxes. Feel free to ask as many questions as it takes to address your interests and concerns, and between the two of you, you should be able to create the plan that best fits your needs and wants!

Most of the tax-saving options can only be accomplished in your lifetime. If you have ceased actively collecting, there are definite advantages to early disposition. If not, there are also some compromise positions that can allow you to enjoy some control of the collection and the tax benefits.

Is Your Collection Worth More Today Than When You Purchased It?

Rare coin collections generally appreciate over time, but there are exceptions. If you bought most of yours in 1980 or 1989 for example, or if you were unfortunate enough to have been the victim of an unscrupulous seller, a current appraisal may show you to be in a loss position. If so and disposition is your intention, you may sell the collection by any method and use the loss to offset an equal amount of capital gains, and you may deduct up to $3,000 of excess capital loss annually as well. If more typically, the collection has appreciated, however, many other issues come into play.

Give Portions of Your Collection to Your Heirs Now

Estate taxes can be punitive. There is an exemption as of 1999 of $650,000 with indexed increases into the future, but tax rates on the balance of your estate could be as much as 55%. You can reduce your taxable estate through gifts to your heirs during your lifetime: $10,000 annually is permissible per recipient without incurring gift taxes. The gift could be appraised portions of your coin collection or other assets.

Recipients must be relatives, but the guidelines are quite liberal. Your advisor will be able to tell you how far the allowance extends.

Donate Your Collection to a Public Charity

If your collection has appreciated, you may be able to enjoy some fiscal benefit while avoiding the trauma of seeing it broken up and sold, through a charitable donation to a public charity. For example, say your cost basis in your qualifying collection was $10,000, but the current fair market value is $60,000. You donate the collection to a qualifying charity. If you are in the 39.6% tax bracket, your tax savings are $23,760... still a great improvement on your basis with all the positive intangibles of charitable giving! Here's what it takes to qualify:

- The collection is qualified capital gain property – this means essentially that everything included has been in the collection for at least a year, was not created by you, nor was it a gift from the creator. The last portions of those qualifications are based on art law, but if you have medallic art or other privately issued exonumia in your collection, they might apply.

- The donee organization is a qualified public charity – public charities generally receive at least part of their support from the public. Examples might be churches, schools, museums and so on. Private foundations, on the other hand, do not qualify for the deduction of fair market value for your collection. You would need verification from the intended donee on its exemption ruling under both section 501(C)(3) and section 509(A). Typically, you will only receive a deduction of your cost for a donation to a private charity versus full fair market value for a donation made to a public charity.

- The donee organization must be able to make "related use" of your donation – your gift of tangible personal property must relate to the donee organization's mission or purpose that resulted in their section 501 exemption. For example, you could donate your coin collection to the ANA or ANS to expand their museum collections and receive a deduction of fair market value. Obviously, a coin collection would relate to missions of increasing the knowledge and enjoyment of coin collecting. You could not donate the collection to a hospital and deduct the fair market value – the deduction would be reduced by 100% of the appreciation above your cost.

- The collection has a "qualified appraisal." – Essentially, a qualified appraisal is one that is performed by a "qualified appraiser." That is an individual who holds himself out to the public as an appraiser and who is expert in the particular type of property being evaluated; is cognizant of the civil penalties possible for a fraudulent overstatement of value; and is totally independent of the property and parties to the donation. There is a checklist of information required that your advisor and appraiser will be familiar with.

Your advisor will also counsel you on allowable percentages of your contribution base, section 68 limitations, and possible Alternative Minimum Tax consequences.

Donate a Fractional Interest in Your Collection to a Public Charity

Don't want to give up your collection interests, but still want some tax relief now? You might consider donating an undivided fractional interest in your collection to a qualified charity. Let's say, for example, that you donate one half interest in the collection to a qualifying museum. Each of you gets to keep the collection for six months of each year and you get to deduct half the fair market value of the collection in the year of the donation. This would be ideal if you collect during the cooler months, but gravitate toward the outdoors in summertime. This is also a good technique of charitable contribution when your contribution base (adjusted gross income) is not large enough to support the entire donation because of percentage limitations.

Some donors structure their contribution to give, say 25% of their collection now, 25% in five years, a third 25% in ten years and the remainder at their death. Any percentage of the collection not donated will become part of your estate. If you perceive the possibility of friction between the charity and your heirs over the remaining divided interest, you may wish to complete the donation as part of your will. This method also allows the value of the collection to continue appreciating, so each subsequent donation may be for a greater amount than the previous ones. Interim appraisals would, of course, be necessary.

Charitable Remainder Trusts

A charitable remainder trust is of great value if you are in need of both income and a tax deduction, and are prepared to give up your collection now. It is particularly advantageous if the collection has enjoyed significant appreciation since purchase. In this arrangement, the donation is made to the qualifying charity in trust. The charity agrees to pay you annually either a fixed amount of money (annuity trust) or a percentage of the trust's total value (unitrust) for life or for a set number of years (not to exceed 20).

The benefit is that if you sold the collection yourself to create income, the principal amount would be reduced by taxes on the capital gains. The trustee can sell the collection tax-free and create a larger principal base. You can also claim the collection's cost as a charitable deduction in the year that the trust is initiated (you cannot claim "fair market value" because the sale disqualifies the greater deduction under the "related use" clause). You receive your agreed-upon payments and when the trust period is complete, all remaining interest in the trust passes to the charity.

There are some caveats. Coins are not "income producing assets," so the collection (or at least most of it) must be sold in the first year of the trust to fund it with qualifying financial vehicles. The annual distribution to the donor must be a minimum of 5% of the trust's value and a maximum of 50%. Additionally, at the conclusion of the agreement, the remainder to the charity must be at least 10% of the initial value. These rules create a certain amount of latitude in the trust agreement that must be negotiated between the donor and the charity. Again, we strongly recommend that you use the services of a competent attorney or tax advisor to represent you.

In summary, there are many options available to you, each with specific benefits and pitfalls. We've stated this several times previously, but we can't reiterate enough: **engage a professional to assist you!**

If you are the surviving spouse of the deceased, exemptions generally allow the estate to pass without tax. The *estate planning* burden then becomes yours, however, as the same exemptions will not apply at your death unless you remarry. If this eventuality was not already considered in your planning, you should contact an estate or tax professional without delay. Even if the survivor's position was considered in the original planning, it cannot hurt to re-evaluate the situation with your attorney.

TIPS FOR HEIRS   As an heir to a taxable estate, most of your opportunities for tax abatement are past. If you are privy to the will of your parent (or other person to whom you will be an heir), perhaps you can advise them to seek counsel if it is obvious from what you've read that the need exists. After the fact, you can only exercise a little damage control. If it is necessary to liquidate all or part of the coin collection to pay estate taxes, the expenses of that liquidation (shipping, auction fees, commissions, etc.) should be deductible from the estate. It is often much simpler to buy a paid-up life insurance policy to cover the tax. Again, a tax professional is well worth consulting.

PART 3
EVALUATING YOUR COLLECTION

CHAPTER 7 – THIRD PARTY AUTHENTICATION AND GRADING

"To 'slab' or not to 'slab,' that is the question."

A Short History of Third Party Authentication and Grading

Once upon a time (up to about 1970 or so), coin collecting was primarily a quiet hobby. Mostly, it interested only those people who enjoyed the study of history through coinage and were motivated toward set completion at whatever level their budgets allowed. It wasn't until late 1972 that one of the five 1913 Liberty nickels became the first coin to bring $100,000, followed soon after by an uncirculated 1794 dollar at $110,000. All of a sudden, rare coins were a collectible to be reckoned with! The grading system of the time allowed for two mint state grades, uncirculated (UNC) and brilliant uncirculated (BU), and up to that point, they had been enough!

The next precipitating event came when Richard Nixon signed a bill allowing America's gold reserves to float free on the international markets. A subset of the bill was that individual Americans could again own gold without restriction for the first time since 1933. Gold coins that had "fled" to Europe and around the world forty years earlier came flooding back. Unfortunately, a large quantity of counterfeit gold coins came with them.

In 1972, the American Numismatic Association opened a certification service (ANACS) to authenticate coins, and over the next fifteen years built the nation's most comprehensive file of genuine and counterfeit coin characteristics. Coins were submitted to the service for a fee and genuine coins were returned with a photo certificate attesting to their authenticity. In the process, a large portion of the counterfeit coins were identified and removed from the marketplace.

Stepping back... in the wake of Watergate and the Arab oil embargo the economy suffered first a recession and then several years of double-digit inflation. Traditional investments were in shambles and in the search for profitable alternatives, rare coins began to be referred to in discussions concerning tangible assets, along with real estate, fine art, stamps, antiques, and other collectibles.

Rare coins are traded in a very thin market when compared to Wall Street's usual offerings. The very essence of rare coins is that the traditionally desirable pieces are in short supply. Certainly there was nowhere near a sufficient supply to meet the demand created by the inflationary economy and new buyers in the coin market. Rare coin prices soared, but as existing saleable inventory was rapidly sold out of the market, it was obvious that something would have to be done.

The professional numismatic community is similar to the art, jewelry, and antique markets in recognizing "condition rarity." This concept, which states simply that when two coins of the same issue trade, the one with the superior state of preservation will realize a higher price, has always existed. It had never been fiscally significant, however, because only a relatively few (and usually very rare) coins showed a wide "spread" of values between adjacent grades.

The American Numismatic Association adopted Sheldon's 70 point grading system and between 1973 and 1977 worked to establish standards for all series under the leadership of numismatic luminary Abe Kosoff. Experts from all coin specialties collaborated with Mr. Kosoff, and the first official ANA grading guide was published in the 1977-1978 time frame. Initially, it recognized three grades to evaluate Mint State coins: Uncirculated or MS-60; Choice Uncirculated or MS-65; and Perfect Uncirculated or MS-70. Unfortunately, the third grade (MS-70) was mostly theoretical, and the two remaining designations quickly proved inadequate for the marketplace. MS-63 (Select Uncirculated) and MS-67 (Gem Uncirculated) were added and worked for awhile before the demand for closer evaluation demanded even more grades. Eventually, all numbers between MS-60 and MS-70 were employed and the adjectival equivalents dropped.

The question quickly arose who would arbitrate these new and complicated standards. Numismatists have always acknowledged that grading is an art and subject to differences of opinion based on relative skill, ownership, and motivation. When the price differences between adjacent grades (the "spread") often became multiples, many buyers were unwilling to pay for the higher grade if they had any question about either the coin or the seller.

In 1978, ANACS added grading to their list of services, annotating (split) obverse and reverse grades on the photo-certificate. Each coin submitted for grading was viewed by a number of staff numismatists (usually 3-4) and the written opinion represented the consensus of the group. The original concept was that ANACS would resolve disputes where a difference of opinion existed. The professional community, however, recognized an opportunity and almost immediately took the program to the next step. They submitted the significant coins in their inventories for grading before offering them to their customers, thus arbitrating the transaction in advance! There have been both disagreements and improvements along the way, but this fundamental concept is as popular today as it was then. Everyone is a little more comfortable when a third-party has rendered an unbiased opinion.

The next significant innovations in third party grading came in 1986, and again, they changed the way that the coin market did business. The Professional Coin Grading Service (PCGS) opened for business in California and offered the combination of placing the consensus-graded coins in ultrasonically sealed holders with a dealer network that would make sight-unseen markets for the coins PCGS graded. Sight-unseen means that the bidding market maker would purchase any PCGS graded example of the issue and grade without regard to what the coin actually looked like. The following year, the Numismatic Guaranty Corporation (NGC) opened on the opposite coast, offering a similar program and features. Almost overnight, the demand for photo-certified coins all but disappeared. By sealing the coins in plastic, the issues of switched coins and mishandling a coin after grading were eliminated. Shortly after the first examples began to show up at coin shows, some wag remarked that with the information cards on top, there was some resemblance to a tombstone. A friend agreed and said they look like little "slabs," and the nickname stuck.

Humor aside, it was a monumental occasion for the coin market. Finally, numismatics had a fixed grade product that could be tracked and traded much like a commodity. In the ensuing years, both NGC and PCGS have gained wide market acceptance, and though other third-party grading services have come and/or gone in the interim, NGC and PCGS remain the acknowledged leaders. The secret of their success is that to date, they alone have maintained sufficient dealer confidence to be traded routinely on a sight-unseen basis. As such, while we will list the contact information for several grading services in the Appendix, we will only address NGC and PCGS in the text.

What Coins Do You Certify?

Certification is an expensive proposition that should not be entered into hastily. At $15-$85 a coin, the total bill for even a small collection can easily run into the thousands of dollars. Few people are readily prepared to make that kind of commitment and rightly so, for not all coins benefit equally from being certified. The rule of thumb, of course, is that the finished product has to be worth more than the raw coin plus the certification fee. But just what does that mean?

There is only one practical reason to certify a coin: to add value, plain and simple! When a dealer (or any astute numismatist for that matter) is looking to buy an uncertified coin, he is trying to guess what the grading service is going to grade it, always giving himself the benefit of the doubt in case of error. For example, if a dealer is looking at your 1886-O Morgan dollar and he is trying to decide whether NGC is going to grade it an MS-63 (bid $1,780) or MS-64 (bid $5,300), he is going to figure it as an MS-63 coin to be on the safe side, and offer a price commensurate with an MS-63 coin. This is only fair, as the alternative would leave him with both the risk and the expense, and that is not a formula that works in business. You, however, could have the coin certified before attempting to sell it. Your upside is that if the grading service calls it an MS-64, you have a $5,300 coin. The downside is the cost of the grading fee. The bottom line is that this issue has a significant spread between grades and (in our opinion) the risk is worth the expense.

That is not always the case. One contrary example would be an uncirculated 1884-CC silver dollar. The coin routinely trades for $75 without certification. In the current market, certified MS-63 examples bid $78 and MS-64s bid $88. With a $15.00 certification fee, it would make no sense to certify this issue unless the coin had a reasonable shot at grading MS-65, which currently bids $210.

One other certification issue to be addressed is "No Grades." One of the factors that has allowed continued market confidence and sight-unseen bidding is the omission of "problem coins" from the product mix. Neither NGC nor PCGS will provide a regular certification for coins that are counterfeit or altered; physically or environmentally damaged; chemically or mechanically cleaned; or coins with significant mint-made, pre-strike defects. If you submit such a coin, the grading service will return it in a poly bag and flip (known in the industry as a "body bag") along with the reason they declined to grade it; they will not, however, return your money.

SUBMITTING YOUR COINS

NGC and PCGS both operate primarily through authorized dealer networks. Most of these dealers will gladly submit your coins to their respective grading services on your behalf. The dealer is compensated with a rebate of approximately 20% of the grading fee. Don't ask him for part of the rebate, but do ask him to preview the coins and help you decide which coins to certify. Most authorized dealers are familiar with both services' standards and can warn you off submitting the coins that are most likely headed for a "body bag."

If you live within driving distance of an authorized dealer, make an appointment to be sure he is available to preview them. If you are not within a reasonable driving distance, you may ship your coins to an authorized dealer of your choice. As this situation adds an additional element of trust, you should pick someone you can feel comfortable with. A good rule of thumb is to select an authorized dealer who is also a member of the Professional Numismatists Guild (PNG). The PNG is the most prestigious numismatic fraternal organization because each new candidate must undergo a detailed background check and be approved by the entire membership. They must then operate under a strict Code of

Ethics and accept binding arbitration in the event of disputes. Contact information for the PNG is also included in the Appendix.

Once you have made your selection of a dealer, call and discuss your intentions and arrangements. You should expect to pay the certification fees and appropriate shipping fees for all legs the coins travel.

WHICH GRADING SERVICE DO I USE?

That is not a simple question. Since humans rather than a computer do grading, it's an inexact art, not a science. Despite the many grades in the system, a coin may still be marginal, solid or superior for a grade. The same person may see the same coin differently on different occasions. For myriad reasons, a grader may see a coin as superior for one grade today and marginal for the next higher grade tomorrow. The consensus grading system ameliorates this phenomenon somewhat, but with the volume of coins graded, there is always some percentage of coins that "could go either way."

Similarly, one group of graders may like a particular "look" more or less than another group and have a slightly different standard "line." This can be a very minute difference, but when it is perceived in the marketplace that there is a disparity in the standards, coins graded by the perceived "tighter" service will reflect a premium in the pricing guides. When this occurs, too many people get wrapped up in the concept that one service is "better" than the other. The reality is that the seasoned numismatists in the marketplace recognize a difference and adjust the values accordingly, no less, no more. They also recognize that where there is variance, there is opportunity. For example, let's take the 1886-O Morgan dollar we were discussing. You're absolutely certain it's either MS-63 or MS-64. If the bid for a PCGS MS-64 is $5,300 and an NGC MS-64 is only bid at $4,900, there is probably a perception in the marketplace that it's a little easier to get an MS-64 at NGC, and that is where you want to send your coin first! If it grades MS-64 at NGC, you have captured most of your grading gain and can then decide whether you wish to spend an additional fee to attempt to "cross-over" the coin to PCGS for the extra $400. If it does not grade at the "easier" service, you may have to reconsider your options at the MS-63 level.

DECLARING SUBMISSION VALUE FOR INSURANCE

When you prepare to submit your coins for grading, you will be asked to declare a value for insurance purposes in case the package is lost or the coins damaged either in transit or at the grading service. Since grading and shipping fees are impacted by this decision, you need to weigh the value ranges of the service levels with the likelihood of loss or damage, then select a liberal, yet realistic value for the coins. For example, you hope the 1886-O Morgan dollar will grade MS-64, but you're not sure. You're also trying to keep your grading fees minimal and time is not an issue. If you valued the coin at the full $5,300 bid, you would have to submit the coin on Express service at $50.00, whereas if you value it at less than $5,000, you could submit the coin for Regular service at $28.00. A list of service costs and value ranges is included, but unless you are an advanced numismatist who is both familiar with grading and market values, you would be wise to ask the authorized dealer for assistance in assigning values. Loss and damage are infrequent occurrences for which you should be fairly compensated, but over-insuring is likely to just increase your expenses.

SERVICE LEVELS

NGC and PCGS both offer similar levels of service based on the premise that the more valuable the coin, the higher the fee. Similarly, if you want a less expensive coin back quicker than the norm, you should be willing to pay more for the speedy service. As such, each level of service has a maximum value, but no minimum.

WALK THROUGH or 1 Day
This highest level of service is usually performed for customers dropping the coins off at the service or at shows. Coins are available for pickup or shipped same day if received by a fixed time deadline, otherwise out the following day. Costs $125 per coin. There is no value cap for this service.

DISPATCH or 3 Day
The second tier also has no maximum value, but is typically used for coins with five-figure price tags. Guaranteed turnaround is one - three business days. Costs $85 per coin.

EXPRESS or 5 Day
This service is only available for coins valued up to $10,000. Cost is $50 per coin and guarantees turnaround in five business days.

EARLYBIRD or REGULAR
This standard service is for coins valued up to $5,000. Cost is $28 - $30 per coin and takes twelve - fifteen business days.

ECONOMY (both services)
Cost is $15 per coin and is available for coins valued up to $300. Economy coins generally take between four and six weeks to turnaround depending on which grading service and their business flow at that time.

GOLDRUSH or BULLION GOLD
This service is the one exception to the rule, as it acknowledges the need for lower cost service combined with speed for low-margin gold pieces valued up to $1,000. Costs $19 - $20 per coin and generally takes five business days. Allowed series are $5 Liberty, $10 Liberty and $10 Indian, $20 Liberty and $20 Saint-Gaudens. PCGS also accepts $5 Indian pieces.

Both NGC & PCGS also offer re-grading for coins they have previously graded and encapsulated, and crossover for coins in the holder of another grading service. Coins are graded with the previous grade covered and the consensus matched to the request by administrative personnel. Fees for both services are assessed at the same pricing levels as regular submissions and retained whether or not the requested action could be accomplished. The benefit of these services is that the grade cannot go down. At the worst, you will be out your expenses and returned the coins as you sent them.

WHEN YOUR COINS COME BACK GRADED

The big day is finally here. You have waited in anticipation of what the grading service thought about your coins, and now you know.

Most likely, you had an idea of what you thought the coins would grade. Chances are, some of the results are higher, some lower, and the majority of them are what you thought they would be. You're pleased for the most part, but what do you do with the coins you think graded lower than they should have? If you submitted the coins through an authorized dealer, you may want him to look over the results and discuss them with you.

If he concurs with your opinion, you may wish to send the coin back for re-grade, guaranteed review or try the other service. Is it worth spending another grading fee? Well, it certainly may be if the coin upgrades and the spreads are wide, but you have to be prepared for it to stay the same, as it does more often than not. Many dealers re-submit the same coin five, ten, even twenty times if the spread merits it and they're convinced of its potential. Sometimes they "hit," but sometimes they just spend thousands in fees before admitting their initial assessment was in error. It's not the end of the world, however. See Chapter 11 titled "Selling Your Collection At Auction" for tips on getting the top dollar for PQ coins that didn't make the higher grade!

In summary, 3rd party grading is an integral part of the rare coin market, but mostly for "commodity" issues and coins where large spreads exist and certification is necessary to get the higher value. Learn how the system can benefit you and what its limitations are, then use it to your maximum advantage.

TIPS FOR HEIRS As a non-collector, getting 3rd party grading for the significant coins in your inheritance may give you a far greater comfort level in assessing the real value of the collection. Because you are probably unfamiliar with the "language" of the hobby, to say nothing of the nuances, we recommend that you spend additional time in qualifying the authorized dealer you take the coins to. Speak plainly as to what your goals are and ask lots of questions. If you're not sure about what an answer means, don't hesitate to say so and ask for a more detailed explanation. You can't know too much about your inheritance; only knowing too little can hurt you!

CHAPTER 8 – GETTING YOUR COLLECTION APPRAISED

"A rose is a rose is a gladiola?"

Need an appraisal? Your personal records will usually give you a pretty good idea of what your coin collection is worth (particularly if you have one of the software programs), but there are several occasions where you may need a formal appraisal to meet some specific need. Requirements vary, and your understanding of them will help you get enough service for the situation without paying too much in appraisal fees.

INSURANCE APPRAISAL

You should insure your coin collection whether you keep it in a safe-deposit box or at home, and particularly if you exhibit or trade portions of it at coin shows. Your insurance company will probably want an appraisal prior to granting coverage, but even if they don't, it may be in your best interests to secure one. The premiums will be assessed on your stated value, but should there be a claim and the research reveals the values were overstated, you will not get the degree of coverage you paid for. Just as with jewels, fine art, or furs, if you over-insure your property, all you accomplish is making the insurance company wealthier.

An insurance appraisal should be figured at replacement cost – the price you would have to pay if you went out and replaced the collection buying from dealers or at auction. It should not matter whether you paid $10,000 for the collection or $200,000; if it would cost $100,000 to replace it today, that's exactly how much you should insure it for. The pertinent point here is that this is a retail appraisal, probably the only instance in which that is most beneficial to the owner. You should make sure the appraiser understands that the purpose is for insurance, as most appraisals are for liquidation value.

Premiums vary by company, but by far, the cheapest coverage is in force when your collection is always in a safe-deposit box. This may seem unnecessary, but in the 1980s, a friend's substantial collection was stolen from his safe-deposit box when a large bank in Boston was broken into over the weekend. Rare, but it happens. Another client's bank vault was flooded for five entire days! Figure to pay one-half % for annual safe-deposit box coverage ($500 for $100,000) and at least double that if you want coverage outside the bank. Special circumstances may require additional premiums, so read the policy language carefully for exceptions and ask however many questions you feel are necessary for you to fully understand the policy.

DATE OF DEATH APPRAISAL

If a coin collection is an asset of a recently deceased person, the value of that collection must be included when completing the estate tax return. An appraisal of the value of the collection at the date of death is required. The IRS stipulates that the "bulk sale method" appraisal should be used. In other words, what the collection would have brought if sold in one bulk sale to a dealer on the date of death. This is very important, especially for valuable collections that are part of large estates, and is a benefit to the heirs.

If a dealer would buy the entire collection outright for $100,000, that is the value that should be used for the date of death appraisal. The benefit is that if the collection is sold at a large public auction held at a location where many collectors and dealers can attend, it could easily bring $130,000 - $150,000. However, for the purposes of estate taxes, which could be as much as 55% on estates valued above $1,000,000, the applicable percentage is only levied against the $100,000. If you end up consigning the collection to auction or shop it around for the best offer, you would only be responsible for the much lower capital gains rate on the amount over $100,000. Consult your attorney or tax advisor.

APPRAISAL FOR DIVORCE

If you are getting a divorce and a coin collection is among the marital assets, you will most likely be required to get it appraised. Finances allowing, one party may want to keep the collection rather than have it sold and the proceeds divided. This will create one more conflict during the divorce. The spouse wanting to keep the collection will hope for a low appraisal, while the selling spouse will hope for a higher one. The fairest way to obtain a Divorce Appraisal is to take the collection to two or three reputable coin dealers (three is optimal, but may be unnecessary and expensive if the first two are within 20% of each other). Tell each dealer you need a written appraisal of what they would pay to buy the collection outright. Expect the appraisal/offer to have a time limit of as little as one week, and to be tied to the spot prices of gold and silver if bullion coins are included.

Assuming that the collection is not to be split up, a "one figure" appraisal (e.g. the sum total offer is $20,000) should be sufficient versus pages of individual offers that would increase the appraisal cost unnecessarily.

SELECTING AN APPRAISER

Selecting the appraiser is the most important part of the process. You are looking for someone who will represent your best interests in providing a knowledgeable and honest evaluation of your collection. Further, the evaluation should match the needs of the situation it is addressing. That said, you still need to maintain the responsibility of looking out for your own interests.

Your appraiser should be a life member of the American Numismatic Association (ANA), a member of the Professional Numismatists Guild (PNG), be established for at least five years (and preferably ten) in the same area, have financial references from a reliable bank and have a solid reputation with knowledgeable collectors. This is ideal. Depending on your location and the relative value of your collection, you may choose (or have) to settle for less, but these are the qualifications you should be seeking. If you have a significant collection, it is probably in your best interests to incur higher expenses (if necessary) to engage an appraiser at this level. Remember, such expenses are usually deductible.

WHAT WILL IT COST?

A formal appraisal can be an expensive undertaking, but the important considerations are that it's done right and that the expense is appropriate relative to the value of the collection. Expect to pay $100 an hour on average. Some small town dealers charge $50 - $75 per hour, dealers in large cities or "high rent" districts tend to charge $125 - $150 per hour, so $100 is a good average. If the collection is significant and the material is rare or esoteric, or if the situation is complex or unusually contentious, you may need the services of a top-rate professional. Their rates can rival that of a law firm's $250 - $500 per hour. We would emphasize, however, that such a level of expertise is usually not necessary for most collections.

In qualifying a dealer, ask for an approximate charge after discussing the scope and purpose of the appraisal. If the dealer won't commit to a figure (say "2-3 hours, no more than 3," for example), find someone else who will. Remember, a "one price," liquidation appraisal will require a lot less time (and expense) than a line by line, individually-bid "grocery list." You may not even have to pay for the former at all. Some dealers will give you a dated, written offer to purchase your coins on a no-obligation basis. Unless you need insurance appraisal values, that offer would suffice as a liquidation appraisal. Others may charge you for a written appraisal with the proviso that if you sell them the collection by an arbitrary date, the appraisal fees will be rebated. Dealers would much rather buy collections than appraise them and you can use that leverage to your advantage. In all fairness, however, if someone does a "free" appraisal, you should at least give them the opportunity to bid when you make a decision to sell.

SAFETY OF THE COINS DURING APPRAISAL

It is your responsibility to ensure the safety of your coins during the appraisal. You should expect it to cost more, but once you have selected an appraiser, the safest method is to have the appraiser come to your bank. A true professional will make an inventory if one does not already exist and then make grading evaluation notes right there in the tiny safe-deposit room. The appraiser will then take the copious notes back to his office to determine values and assemble the appraisal. Tell the appraiser when you need it, and don't forget to ask for an estimate on time. Even a modest collection, appraised under these ideal conditions (ideal for you, but NOT necessarily for the dealer) will probably be charged at 10 hours or so.

A less expensive alternative is to take the coins to the dealer and sit with the coins while the appraisal notes are being made, returning at an agreed upon date to pick up the appraisal. If your location or schedule requires you to either ship or leave your collection for appraisal, you should put a little more effort into qualifying your appraiser. This is simply good business and a natural step in assuring the safety of your coins.

In summary, determine the scope of your collection and what you are trying to accomplish with an appraisal, select the professional who combines the qualifications and economies best suited to your situation, and safeguard your collection during the process.

TIPS FOR HEIRS Once again, the physical issues here are not specific to numismatists and the guidance in the chapter should be as understandable as it is pertinent. If you have created a basic inventory where none existed previously, try to get a "ball park" estimate of the collection's worth in your initial discussion with potential appraisers. Because grading is such an issue, they may be reluctant. They should, however, be able to tell if you're dealing with a few hundred, a few thousand, or something really significant. That information should help you gauge the economies of the process. At that point, we would recommend that you spend a little more time qualifying your appraiser if you are not a coin collector and are unfamiliar with "who's who" in the marketplace.

PART 4
DISPOSING OF YOUR COLLECTION

CHAPTER 9 - SELLING YOUR COLLECTION THROUGH OUTRIGHT SALE

"Liquidation price means low enough that the buyer feels comfortable with even the coins he didn't want."

This chapter is the first of three that outline methods for disposing of your collection. Each has benefits for certain types of coins, and weaknesses for others. The common thread is that each method subscribes to the philosophy that "time is money." Simply put, this means that all other things being equal, the faster you get paid for your collection, the less you are likely to receive. This is not an unfair situation, as you should come to see in these chapters. We are going to try to put you inside the heads of your potential customers, and help you understand their motivations for buying. Their time is valuable, as is yours. Our goal is to aid you in making a measured decision of how much time you are willing to invest in the disposition process.

Outright sale is without question the easiest method of selling a whole or partial collection. You present the coins to one or more buyers. They make offers. You accept or decline. Your time invested is limited to the period you are with the coins at the evaluation(s); if you accept an offer, you receive your payment and get on with your life. If you assembled the collection, this may either be devastating or cathartic, but it won't drag out any agony. You probably also have some idea of what you think the collection should bring, but in making this estimate, did you try to consider what you would be thinking if you were sitting on the other side of the table?

First, we will assume that you are offering any collection of substance to a coin dealer. Dealers are most likely to have both the motivation and wherewithal to buy an entire collection. It is also easier to locate them through their advertising and they can be qualified through their references and affiliations. What is the dealer thinking when you bring him your collection to bid?

Coin dealers are in business to buy collections coming through the front door (or through the mail). Most of their advertising and their longevity at a particular site are planned specifically to entice just such a situation. Face it, coins are a fixed supply commodity. If you're in the business, you have to buy to have product to sell, and advantageous buying is at the core of every successful coin business. The coin dealer wants to buy your collection – it's his *raison d'être* – and the nicer the collection, the more he wants it.

We have two parties together; one who wants to sell and one who wants to buy. Now comes the sticking point. In any trading situation, the final result reflects the combination of knowledge and leverage of the parties. The dealer wants to buy the collection at the lowest price he can pay without it walking out the door. His leverage is that he has the money and willingness to buy the whole deal, plus any degree of impatience that you possess or he can instill in you. You may also believe that he is more knowledgeable about current markets than you are. You, nonetheless, want to feel that you are getting the maximum reasonable price for your coins. Your leverage is that he does not want to let you out the door with the collection… plus your displayed numismatic knowledge and negotiating skills.

A dealer is bidding on three planes when a collection is offered. First, there are those coins for which he knows he has customers or which are readily liquid in his retail or "high wholesale" operations. These will generally be figured strongly because his risk and expense of holding inventory is minimal. Second are the coins that do not fit that criteria – coins that are not routinely traded and which will require some effort to find a wholesale buyer who will then have all the leverage in a subsequent trade. This particularly applies to bulk where additional· shipping weight is also a factor. These coins will be figured cheaply because of the effort and expense necessary to resell them at a profit. This may seem callous, but it's a matter of perspective. The proof sets you bought the years your children were born are probably very special to you. Those same proof sets sitting unsold on a dealer's shelf are merely inventory that is losing (or costing) interest. He will take the time to find the "high buyer" because it's how he makes his living, but his bid for those coins will reflect both his intent to make a profit at wholesale, and any uncertainty about the high buyer and his buying levels. The third factor is not coin related, but rather what the dealer perceives his competition to be. If you live in a small town with only one coin dealer, his basic assumption may be that he pretty much has things his own way. This may also apply in any locale if the dealer perceives you aren't "shopping." Lacking any evidence of competition, his bid is simply not likely to be as motivated.

There are those who will read the last paragraph and mumble about "rip-off" coin dealers, but the reality is endemic throughout society and business in general, not just this small portion of it; it lies at the very heart of Capitalism. Americans as a whole are not raised to function in a barter system or to be negotiators. We go to the store and buy what we want at the marked price, only sometimes, perhaps, after checking the newspapers for sales. It's what we see in childhood and by the time we are adults making our own decisions, most of us are conditioned to the process. As a result, a large percentage of people still pay "sticker price" even in those environments where some negotiating is expected.

When selling or trading something in, the same conditioning applies – the dealer establishes the market and as the perceived authority figure, a surprisingly large number of people accept that quote as fact…or at least believe that their only options are yes or no. The dealer, of course, falls into that group of people who, through aptitude or training, are both comfortable and practiced in negotiating (that is, appearing not to be negotiating). At a minimum, you need to present your collection and your business skills in their best light if you want to get a better price for your coins.

Here are some tips for negotiating the best deal on your collection:

- Know the Best Coins for Direct Sale
  Premium money is generally found in areas of uncertainty. Categories where no question of upgrade or signature rarity exists generally trade easily within well-defined boundaries. These include low premium gold coins that have small spreads between

buy and sell prices, saleable "collector coins" that are solid for their grade or have no more than modest spreads between adjacent grades, and in some cases, "bulk" coins (if real wholesale markets are known to both parties). These coins are usually best sold directly with as little muss and fuss as possible. To get the best prices from direct sale, particularly if you expand beyond these "best" categories consider all of the following tips and how you might apply them to your effort.

- Allow yourself a National Marketplace
  The world has become a much smaller place through increasingly more rapid communications and transport. You need not limit your search for outlets to your hometown… and if your collection is significant enough, the outlets will come to you!

- Find a "Full Service" Dealer
  Remember the note about liquidity-based bidding. A large dealer with a wide clientele and business contacts will "see" your more common coins as more liquid because they routinely sell that kind of material as well as the "good" coins. They already know who the high buyer is and what they're paying. Additionally, because of their business volume, they will not have the need (nor temptation) to "make their month" on your collection. As a result, they're more likely to bid the whole deal "closer."

- Create an "Aura of Competition"
  It is rarely a bad idea to get more than one bid on something you're selling and NEVER a bad idea to let a potential buyer know that other people are bidding (whether they are or not). This can be communicated after you get a bid – "Is this your best offer, Mr. Smith? I know dealers sometimes leave a little 'wiggle room,' but I have two other people bidding and this isn't that kind of negotiation" – or before – "I want you to know in advance, Mr. Smith, that I'm offering the collection for bid to three people. Please give me your best offer the first time."

- Display your knowledge in discussing the bid
  Coin people, dealers or otherwise, respect those who speak the language and whom they can relate to. You don't necessarily have to have a deep knowledge if you can "sell" yourself on a

few key points. If you have a few coins in your collection that stand out, bring them up. "What grade did you bid the 95-O dollar at, Mr. Smith?" Similarly, get a feel for the levels being offered for your second tier material. "What percentage of 'sheet' are you paying me for the proof sets?"

- "Play the Player"
  You need not necessarily be a market expert to get the "feel" of a coin collection if you are at all adept at reading others. Follow up the responses to the questions above with some resistance or qualification and see what kind of response you get. "You bid the 95-O as AU-58? Wouldn't I be better off to try to certify it and see if they'd grade it mint state before I sell it?"...or "You're only paying XX% on the proof sets? Isn't that a little low?" In either case, what you're looking for is not really any specific response, but the logic and timing of it. If the dealer can immediately address the questions with logic and weigh options, he may be extremely glib, but more likely he is comfortable with his offer. Alternatively, if he's evasive or there's no logic to his response, there's very likely negotiating room left in the offer.

- Split the Deal
  Rather than offer the whole collection in one lot, offer "test" groups for bid to get a feel for your potential buyers. Generally, there is more control when dealing with smaller, manageable "pieces" and you can often get a bit more in this manner. There is also the "bait" technique of letting the bidders know that there is more beyond. This perception may lead some bidders to treat you better in the early rounds. The trade-off is more of your time.

In summary, only you can decide how much of your time you are willing to invest in the disposition of your collection. Generally, the more productive time spent, the better the result. You can be most effective in preparing for disposition by knowing your collection, knowing the market and knowing your potential buyers.

TIPS FOR HEIRS If you are a non-collector and after reading this chapter you want to use this method, we would recommend strongly that you seek multiple offers. We would also recommend that you first read and consider the options in the next two chapters as well.

CHAPTER 10 – SELLING YOUR COLLECTION THROUGH AN AGENT

"A good agent is a true blessing."

It may be practical for you or your heirs to use the services of an agent to sell your collection. The objective in choosing this method is to get more money than you would through direct sale. The trade-off (again) is that it will take more time. That said, you might even wish to enlist the services of several agents to sell different parts of your collection.

Many people employ an agent to assist them in selling real estate. The agent knows real estate values, has ways to contact qualified customers, and understands how to deal with them. A good coin dealer has the same qualifications and contacts in his field, but you rarely hear the term agent used in that context. Dealers would generally prefer to purchase coins and collections outright (at the lower price), and then have a free hand to resell them without customer consultation. They will, however, take a collection on consignment rather than let it walk out the door.

A client/agent relationship is a relatively long one. As the owner of multiple properties may commission the real estate agent to dispose of one at a time, so may the owner of a coin collection turn over its elements in groups. This gives the agent a more narrow focus to concentrate on and allows you to maintain control. The key in any case is regular communication and interaction between you and the agent.

Coins that the agent has been given may not sell and be returned. The asking price may need to be adjusted downward. There may be a change in market conditions. While the agent may be doing most of the work, you, the seller, will need to stay involved. As real estate agents and sellers work together as partners to their mutual benefit, so must you and your agent. The agent should be expected to inform you of market conditions and help set prices. Above all, you must be able to trust the agent; to have faith in his ability; and be confident that he is looking after your best interests. One way to gauge this is to test the agent's overall performance with a few coins prior to making any major commitment.

It only makes sense to use an agent if his services result in you receiving a significantly higher sale price for the coins while reducing your personal efforts in concluding the transaction. What, however, constitutes a significantly higher price? This, we suppose, would depend on the value of the collection. Even for an expensive collection, the amount would have to be at least 10% greater than the outright offer (and probably more) to justify the additional time, hassle and expense... probably 20 % - 25% for a smaller collection. You have to consider what kind of circumstances could generate the difference.

A prime example would be a specialized collection where market values are not well known among most dealers and collectors (e.g. a specialist could sell a group of error coins, ancient coins, or Dutch Jetons to best advantage). Your choice should know about the coins, the market and the serious collectors of the specialty. The same coins were probably valued at considerably less as part of the overall collection offer, and would still likely bring less if sold by a dealer who did not specialize in these areas.

Another example would be better coins handpicked for their eye appeal or quality within the grade, particularly where the price spread to the next grade is wide. The agent would first advise you on grading options, possibly getting some of the coins certified in the higher grade with a significant jump in value. An outright buyer would have no such incentive. Even if the coins did not achieve the higher grade, the agent would know which buyers might be enticed to pay a higher price because they also perceived some degree of upgrade potential.

Remember—the agent's role is not just to know the coins, but also the markets and the players—especially the upgrade specialists!

The first step in seeking an agent is to determine the nature of what you plan to sell, then try to match the agent with the product. This may seem obvious, but a common mistake among sellers is to retain unqualified agents. If your coins are specialized, seek a specialist. If your coins are mainstream, look for the following kinds of qualifications:

- Scope of Company – the agent (or his company) routinely handles coins of the same types, grades and values as those in your collection, and has strong customer demand for such coins.

- Grading Service Experience
The agent (or his company) routinely submit coins to the grading services and has a strong feel for where the "standard lines" of the grades are. Ideally, the agent or other personnel in his company will have worked for a grading service and understand both the process and "looks" that are most often rewarded on marginal decisions.

- Regular Show Attendance
The agent (or his company) attends coin shows on a regular basis where routine contact with other numismatists provides an ongoing feel for the market and provides a wide range of business contacts. Taken a step further, attendance on the national show circuit would give even more insight and opportunity.

- Mailing List
The agent (or his company) has an extensive mailing list and will present your coins to the maximum number of potential buyers.

These qualifications promise the potential of significantly higher returns, but you also want to pick an agent who genuinely wants the role. A lot of dealers only want to buy and sell coins, and really don't have the time or inclination to work with you as an agent. You should not be upset if someone you approach turns you down, nor do you want to enlist a reluctant ally. The last thing you need is a dealer who thinks he's doing you a favor by selling your coins for you.

Many variables can influence the arrangement you make; however, five important elements should be negotiated in any event:

- The agent's fees should be discussed and agreed upon in advance. Generally, the agent should receive a percentage of the selling price. This fee is usually graduated and predicated on the value of the coins. You could hardly expect an agent to go to the trouble and expense of selling a $100 coin for a 5% commission. A more equitable arrangement might be a 15% commission on coins valued under $1000 and 10% on coins valued over that amount. That, of course, is a matter of negotiation. If you wish your agent to provide grading advice on your coins, you may need to negotiate a separate deal on any "upgrade profits." This is in your best interests, as it will ensure his grading "eye" is used for your benefit rather than just his own.

- A firm minimum price for each coin or group of coins to be sold should be agreed upon in advance with the understanding that the seller be advised before any coins are sold for less than this fixed price. Turning coins over to an agent and accepting their promise that they will do their best is not acceptable. It could also be expected that the agent might do some research and make a few phone calls prior to suggesting a minimum price. Agents should be prepared to substantiate the values they suggest. Conversely, you should not demand unreasonable minimums. No agent is going to waste his time and energy trying to sell coins that are obviously overpriced. Negotiating the minimums is a critical component of this kind of arrangement. If you are not comfortable with the value range of your individual coins, it may be best to get a written offer first. Then you'll know what you're trying to improve upon before negotiating with an agent.

- The agent should be given the exclusive right to sell the coins for a specific period of time. Depending of the nature of the collection, the agent may have standard practices they wish to follow. Allowing the agent a set length of time to sell the collection should be separated from the payment schedule. Within reason, the owner should be paid as the coins are sold. A good method to use is to make periodic settlements based on time or dollar amount. If the agent is given 90 days to sell the coins, it would seem fair to request that they make payments at thirty and sixty day intervals, or when the amount collected reaches $5000 or more. We would be wary of an agent who didn't agree to this proposal. Requesting periodic payments is also a simple and positive way to measure the agent's performance.

- The agent must agree to be totally responsible for the coins while in his possession. The agent you select may be the most honorable person on earth... but they would still not be immune to theft or natural disaster. Proof of sufficient insurance coverage is mandatory. In many cases, the most prudent plan would still be to give the agent a limited number of coins to sell at any one time.

- Put the agreement in writing. Good contracts make good trading partners, and this is a business arrangement between two parties. All terms must be spelled out and the document signed by both parties in whatever manner creates a binding contract in your state.

One other area where agents can be used is in moving "bulk." Bulk is the bane of most coin dealers' existences. Some customers accumulated ten proof and mint sets a year for forty years and can't understand why the dealer is not enthused when the three wheel barrows full of sets are wheeled through the door. The answers are low price and low margin plus high (relative) weight! We can virtually guarantee you that if you have a lot of this material in your collection, it will generally be bid very low as part of any outright purchase offer... probably 70% to 85% of "sheet." To the dealer's perspective, it is cumbersome, difficult to process and likely to sit gathering dust while more lucrative sales of products are prioritized. Nonetheless, there are a few dealers who specialize in the sale of this kind of material and are the "high buyers." Your agent for this kind of material should know who those high buyers are and be willing to handle the administrative functions of arranging and completing the transactions. In return, he should either receive a mutually agreed fixed fee or perhaps 5% - 10% and expenses. You should still come out ahead of the typical direct sale offer.

In summary, match the agent with the material, establish realistic minimums that make using this method worthwhile, qualify the agent, put the agreement in writing and communicate regularly with the agent throughout the agreement period.

TIPS FOR HEIRS If you are a non-collector and wish to use this option, we recommend that you get an outright purchase offer first. Use extra diligence in qualifying potential agents, and pay close attention in having the agent(s) validate the established minimum prices. Use the direct offers as a comparison and make sure that the minimums offer a significant increase. It may be even more important here to offer small test groups to get comfortable with the process and the agent.

CHAPTER 11 – SELLING YOUR COLLECTION
AT AUCTION

"The auction is the last free marketplace in numismatics."

The ideal situation to sell any product is to get it in front of as many potential customers as possible. When the product is a limited supply item like a rare coin, the key word becomes competing customers and an auction is frequently the best venue to achieve that ideal. There are many benefits to this method of disposition, but the primary one is that in a good auction (one with many bidders), each coin should realize at least its true worth. The trick is in determining those coins that will create the most competition and a result superior to other means of disposition.

The auction is a true free market in which each coin stands on its own merits. Every item is examined carefully by those people most interested in them, and who are willing to back their opinions with their money. If you have a coin that is rare enough that it trades infrequently, its current value would have to be described as uncertain. In an outright purchase of such a coin, most dealers are going to factor that uncertainty into their price unless they absolutely know they have a buyer at a certain level. A well-advertised sale by an established auction house, on the other hand, will likely draw the attention of all the known buyers… and any others as well. The numismatic community is a fairly small one, and most serious buyers are aware when something of interest is offered for sale, particularly at auction. When that condition exists, competitive demand will dictate the strongest result and produce the truest value for that coin.

Similarly, the "perceived grade" of the coin can influence the price realized for any particular coin. We related in some earlier chapters that even the eleven Mint State grades are not sufficient to recognize precise value, particularly where a large price spread exists between adjacent grades. Many auction buyers make an art out of estimating upgrade potential and compete against each other for those "spread" coins. For example, we discussed the 1886-O Morgan dollar being worth $1,780 in MS-63 and $5,300 in MS-64. If a premium example of this issue were offered at auction either "raw" (uncertified), or certified MS-63, interesting things could happen in the bidding. One bidder might call the coin "63.2," thinking the coin had a twenty-percent chance of upgrading. Usually, he would then be willing to bid the $1,780 plus 20% of the difference between $1,780 and $5,300... or roughly $2,500. He is betting his skill and risking an additional 20% in hopes of a 100% return. Another bidder might think the coin has a 40% chance of upgrading and you now have a contest. Compared to an outright offer of the $1,780 bid for the lower grade, this may be a good deal for you, particularly if you were unsuccessful in getting the coin graded higher. The nice thing about coins is that we all see things a little differently and beauty is most certainly in the eye of the beholder.

A third competitive bidding factor is eye-appeal. All coins were not created equal and many people will pay a premium for pieces they consider superior whether the grade reflects that appeal or not. Again, the "beholder" factor can apply. Some looks are almost universally appreciated – sharply struck coins with bright and flashy luster for example – while others, like original mint toning, have a more mixed reception.

Finally, if you have something esoteric – items that are not traded routinely and have infrequently updated pricing guides – a good auction may again bring the very best price. Examples could be issues collected by variety, like large cents and bust halves, world coins, errors, or many categories of exonumia. If you have substantial holdings of these kind of items, choose an auctioneer with a strong track record for the particular genre – one who has the clientele (both mailing list and attendance) and auction locations to put the coins in front of the greatest number of potential buyers.

These factors are what make an auction the best venue for a wide spectrum of coins. Your task is to pick the auctioneer that can put your coins in front of the right people, preferably in quantity. When looking for an auctioneer, you should consider the following qualifications:

- Financial Resources
  An auction consignment is first and foremost a business deal. As with using an agent, an auctioneer must demonstrate sufficient financial resources to ensure your comfort that they can both mount a sale and pay you at the stated settlement date. They must also accept liability and provide full insurance against the loss or damage of your collection.

- Longevity in the business
  The numismatic auction is a multi-faceted business operation that requires a great deal of development before everything flows smoothly... consignor and bidder bases, cataloging references and expertise, site setup and physical security, auction flow and administrative efficiency... plus much, much more. Practice makes perfect is doubly applicable here... because it's your money that's involved! Go with a proven entity.

- Advertising Resources
  Success breeds success. You can't have the top sales without great advertising and vice versa. Look for the companies who are doing the major advertising in the trade papers and on the Internet. They put on the sales that justify the cost of full-page ads... and the bigger the sale, the more bidders to bid on your coins.

- Location
  Like real estate, the first three characteristics of a great coin auction are location, location, and location. A company that is limited to holding auctions in locations out of the mainstream is just not going to draw a large bidder base. Some companies hold auctions in major financial centers with good regional access. Our philosophy is to hold sales in conjunction with major coin shows. Our premise is that most of the major bidders would be in attendance anyway, and more who were not planning to attend will be doubly enticed. An additional benefit to this philosophy

is that there may also be a convenient location so that you can attend and see your own collection cross the auction block.

- Variety of Sales
  Some sales are restricted to certified coins, and may be offered at an auction site, over the Internet, or both. The biggest sales offer both certified and uncertified coins, allow mail, Internet and live public bidding, and generally employ the most extensive cataloging resources.

- Competitive Rates
  Auction companies charge both buyer's and seller's fees to pay the expenses of the sale and turn a profit. A seller's fee of 5% has become standard and you should not have to pay more, unless your collection has extraordinary "bulk" or requires out-of-the ordinary attention. Indeed, if you have a significant collection, you may be able to negotiate a better rate.

- Strong Writing and Imagery
  Catalog descriptions and photography create immediate excitement and demand for a sale's coins and are all that is available to bidders who cannot attend the sale in person. Our company is currently pioneering the use of CD-ROM and the Internet as alternative cataloging media, and this may well become the wave of the future. Until then, look for examples of good catalog writing and high quality photography.

- Professional Personnel
  It takes quality personnel and lots of them to put on a great auction. The auction process is a complex one when done right… consignment coordination, grading advice, cataloging, customer relations. In qualifying auctioneers, be sure to ask them how many people are involved in handling your consignment and what their roles are. Our company provides potential consignors with a video that details the auction process from start to finish, and other companies should at least have literature that covers the same ground. Any company is only as good as its people. Talk to several and get a feel for how they will treat your collection! In summary, auction is usually the best venue for high quality coins whose values are uncertain, particularly if the

coins trade infrequently, or may have some upgrade potential. A good auction draws the right mix of bidders to establish the real value for each individual coin, often far in excess of the average price for the grade.

If this seems the best route for you, interview potential auctioneers to determine who combines the best business resources, numismatic venues and personnel assets!

As an aside, our company has expanded our scope of venues to include several kinds of Internet auctions. The Internet is an amazing communications tool that, among other things, allows individuals to perform functions that previously were only available to businesses. Someone asked, "What if a collector or heir wants to sell their collection by themselves on the Internet?" Well, the many auction web sites like eBay, Yahoo and Amazon are certainly available for just such a project. The question is whether the choice is a good one relative to the other options. We have a good idea of the basics, so consider the following questions:

- Do you already have a "feedback" rating that will give you credibility with the bidder base? Many Internet auction bidders are leery about who they deal with. They are, after all, sending their hard-earned money to someone they've never met and probably never heard of. The equalizer is the feedback system that each Internet auction employs to establish "cyber-reputations." Each party to a "trade" gets the forum to comment on how the other trader performed. Every positive comment equals a point. Every complaint takes one away and the text of the complaint is there for future potential traders to evaluate. If you don't have a feedback rating, some bidders will avoid your auctions altogether and others will bid less (as if ameliorating their risk).

- Do you have the equipment and skill to create digital images of the coins to be auctioned? It's a proven fact that Internet auction items that don't have pictures bring much less money. Disregarding the skills, you will need either a digital camera or a flatbed scanner, and an image management program to acquire the images. You will also need either a web site or learn to use one of the "free posting" sites to upload your images.

- Do you have the skills to write descriptions for each item? Auction bidders are best motivated when a "story" is available to make the coin more interesting. It's called "building value," and the visual image and description provide the combination that maximizes an Internet auctions' results.

- Do you have the business skills to analyze potential problem situations? Can you collect a bad check or determine whether a "special request" from a customer is legitimate or a scam? Most of the people on the Internet are honest, but there are exceptions. Unfortunately, it doesn't take many bad deals to turn a profitable situation into a loss.

- Do you have the knowledge and resources to send high dollar value packages to a hundred different people? There is a lot of administrative responsibility in conducting one's own auctions, not the least of which is delivering the goods! It takes a thorough knowledge of postal regulations and requirements, a considerable amount of shipping materials, and a great deal of organization.

- Do you really want to sell coins that might have upgrade potential in an Internet-only venue? Actually, the question is whether you can recognize the coins that have upgrade potential. The answer to the main question is a resounding, "NO!" Consider again the premium 1886-O dollar in MS-63 that might eventually be graded MS-64 (and worth $5,000 or so). In a live auction where the viewing can be done in person, someone confident in their grading skill might pay $2,500, $3,000, or more. In the Internet only venue, however, no one is going to pay much over the MS-63 "bid" of $1,780 because you cannot confidently determine upgrade potential from a scan.

The final questions are whether you have the time and patience to accomplish this, and whether the outcome is likely to be superior enough to justify your added involvement (which will be considerable). If you can answer yes to all these questions, then maybe this is an option for you to consider and you probably don't need any further guidance from us. If not, we strongly recommend you seek a different option, as these questions just scratch the surface of what can be a complex and diverse process!

TIPS FOR HEIRS A major auction can be the best option for heirs faced with the disposition of a valuable coin collection, particularly if you have no knowledge of numismatics and are concerned about getting fair value. In this scenario, the auctioneer is working on percentage and your best interests are theirs: the more money you make, the more money they make! Additionally, the values will be established by third parties in the competitive bidding process. The real benefit of employing a major auction house is their versatility. Summing up all of the methods of disposition, that certain coins are better suited for one method, while others would benefit more from a different venue. A major company should be willing to recommend the best venue for each of your coins and split the collection to your best advantage. Just be sure to ask!

Chapter 12 – Etiquette & Tips

"Tact is the ability to insult someone in such a manner as
to have them leave smiling."

The purpose of this book is to help you plan for the future and if you wish, to dispose of your coin collection without getting ripped off by the government, coin dealers or other collectors. That's pretty blunt, and not the least bit tactful. We find, however, that most people approach the process with either too much of that attitude or too little.

It's reasonable to assume that you want to receive as much money for your collection as possible. Similarly, it's reasonable to believe that potential buyers would want to pay the least amount they can. The one thing that's absolutely certain is that everyone else will prioritize his or her own interests. You should too! In plain language, it's your ultimate responsibility to make your best deal at some level. Once that's understood, a combination of business and common sense along with a little diplomacy will usually result in an acceptable compromise.

There is a certain etiquette within the numismatic community. Its first premise is the division of roles. If you present yourself as a coin dealer, you are automatically responsible for all your actions and decisions in the numismatic arena. That means if you make a mistake, you live with it. It also imparts a certain level of responsibility toward those who are not dealers. Dealers trade with each other at wholesale levels, in part because they speak a sort of verbal shorthand that assumes a level of expertise. A coin is presented, offered, inspected and purchased (or not) without fanfare, and the principals move on to the next deal.

Conversely, many collectors ask a lot of questions (and rightly so), are nervous about their acquisitions, and return a portion of those purchases after the sale. In return for this extra "maintenance," dealers charge collectors more and pay them less than they would another dealer. It is the way of things, and perfectly justifiable, as there have to be both retail and wholesale levels for any market to function. Naturally, most collectors would like to purchase at wholesale, and occasionally, they get that opportunity. Usually, the key to this is demonstrating a familiarity with wholesale market levels, negotiating pleasantly and well, and asking only pertinent questions.

The same is true on the selling end. If you give the impression that you know what you are doing – are organized, prepared and unlikely to waste the dealer's time, you will get the best bid or options the first time out. We recommend, however, that you do not represent yourself as a dealer. Some collectors claim to be "vest pocket" dealers in hopes of receiving higher offers. Usually, this backfires as the dealer then feels relieved from any obligation to point out unrecognized rare varieties, obvious upgrades or the like. Be who you are, be up front, and be positive.

Any dealer bidding your collection of coins is being offered a valued opportunity to conduct his business. As a non-professional, you should be able to expect:

- An appointment with sufficient time to evaluate your collection.

- Financial and industry references at your request (and you should request them).

- Professional treatment of you and your collection with a mind to both care and security.

- You should ask (prior) that any coins bid at $1,000 or more be identified singly, also that any coins that would benefit from certification be listed.

- A written offer presented in a timely manner. The offer should be dated and any deadline or bullion spot price reference noted.

- If the company has an auction house as well and you request it, recommendations on which coins are better suited for auction or direct sale should also be listed.

- Prompt payment in good funds if the offer is accepted. If the collection is sold at auction, payment in good funds on the settlement date as promised.

The dealer has a right to expect certain conduct from you as well:

- That you keep any scheduled appointment and are prompt. This applies to the dealer and his staff as well.

- The collection should be as organized as possible to minimize the time necessary to evaluate and bid it. Even a basic inventory indicating the location of each item is helpful, as is sequencing the coins by denomination and date. If one group out of the collection contains most of the "value," it can be presented separately.

- You should not "shop" the dealer's offer to other dealers. It's OK to tell each bidder that other bids are being sought, but you should neither reveal what the other bids are nor who's bidding. Shopping an offer for a few more bucks is strictly "bush league" and it can definitely backfire as well. For example, if your first bidder did not make a strong bid and you reveal the number, the second bidder may play the competition instead of the real value and you'll come up short. Similarly, if you reveal whom else you plan to contact, the possibility exists that the bidders could get in contact and collude to your disadvantage. Remember, the aura of unknown competition is the strongest lever you have to inspire the dealers you contact to figure the deal tight and give their best bids.

- You should tell the dealer "yes" or "no" in a reasonable amount of time, and that applies even if you accept another bid. It would be considerate for you to let him know the winning bid. He can learn from the experience and not feel that his time was wasted. That can be to your advantage as well, because if you bring back more coins for him to bid, he should both appreciate your professionalism AND bid higher the next time!

Above all, you should both expect and extend courtesy. Waste little time with a dealer who is discourteous, nor waste time responding. Ask and answer questions, but beware of becoming agitated, even if you disagree with something you hear. Your mission is to get the greatest possible price for your collection, and to accomplish that, it's usually best to reserve judgement until all the information is in! The very person you disagreed with may be the high overall bidder!

As stated before, auction is often the most compelling option for collection disposition. A successful auction achieves the highest gross result for each lot when presented to a wide number of knowledgeable bidders, and especially when your coins are choice quality. Still, there may be some coins where your net result would have been better served in another venue. There is also the fact that many portions of an auction agreement are flexible and should be negotiated. Here are some of the issues and options:

- Ask the auctioneer's consignment coordinator to evaluate your collection and make recommendations on which coins should be auctioned and which would be better sold by another method. Ask him to explain why.

- Do you wish to be recognized for your collecting achievements? If you've been to a numismatic auction, you may have heard it referred to as, say, the "John Smith Sale" or seen the catalog cover proclaim, "The George Brown Collection Sale." In all likelihood, neither Mr. Smith nor Mr. Brown consigned every coin in the sale, but they were recognized as the signature consignor. Sometimes on a smaller scale, a catalog may feature the collections of several signature consignors. Some consignors prefer anonymity, but if you wish the recognition, becoming a signature consignor involves three factors:

1. Your overall collection must be of general significant value. This could vary from auction to auction, but for a rough figure, let's use $250,000.

2. Alternatively, you may have an interesting collection of a more specific focus... possibly something of the nature of a wide accumulation of Sheldon variety Large cents or Overton variety Bust halves. Another angle would be condition rarity. We recently auctioned two sets of Mercury dimes for separate consignors, each which contained many of the finest graded examples.

3. The common thread is that you should ask. If it's a "slam dunk," the auctioneer will probably ask you, but that doesn't mean they will not be receptive otherwise. Be realistic, but don't hesitate to point out your logic, particularly if there's a good story behind the collection!

- Auction companies charge a seller's fee and a buyer's fee to make their expenses and earn a profit. They are motivated to get as much for your coins as possible because they, in turn, will realize greater commissions. With that philosophy in mind, it is then a matter of resources expended on presenting and selling lots. If you have high-dollar, highly desirable single pieces, the auctioneer is much better off than if you have more inexpensive coins or bulk material, even if the total dollar value is the same. Therefore, you can often negotiate a lower seller's fee if you have the "right" kind of material. Other factors also apply. You should, for example, keep in mind that the lowest commission rate is not necessarily the best deal. The first consideration should be the auctioneer's capability to give your collection maximum exposure and promotion. An extra percentage point or two is meaningless if another auctioneer could get an extra 20% for your coins!

- Some people sell their coins unrestricted and others place a "reserve" bid to protect them from bringing what they perceive to be "too little." We believe you should place reserve bids only if you are very familiar with current markets and have good reason to believe that you will easily realize more than the reserve elsewhere if you "buy-back" the lot. Auctioneers also have "reserve" fees, a percentage that you will pay if you do not let the item sell. These are necessary because the auctioneer must make money for their services and a lot that does not sell is a lost opportunity otherwise. Generally, the percentage is based on the overall terms of your consignment and how realistic the auctioneer perceives your reserves to be. You should expect the reserve fee to be 5%-10%. If the amount is more than that, ask for an explanation. If the consignment coordinator says your reserve is too high, you should discuss the rationale carefully. Consignment coordinators are usually very savvy about what works at what levels. If you don't heed their advice, you are gambling at best. Unless you're right, the auctioneer will still earn the reserve fee. You, on the other hand, will still have the coin, but at a higher cost basis. Depending on the overall quality of your consignment, you may be able to negotiate better reserve terms on some or all of your coins.

- Ask the consignment coordinator what the dollar values are for photography and lotting in the auctions you contemplate consigning to. You want the maximum number of photographs and as much descriptive cataloging as possible, and this may vary depending on how much the auctioneer has to pay for the auction venue rights. For example, in some sales, the minimum value for a catalog photograph may be $1,500 and in others, $2,500. The latter sale, while possibly a better venue overall, might not be as good for your coins valued $1,500 - $2,400! Similarly, each sale will have a minimum lot value. In some cases, it's $250, some $500, and in the very best of sales, it may be $1,000. Most auction companies will allow you to combine coins to reach the minimum, but there is a limit to the number that may be used and still get individual, mainstream placement! Our company cuts it off at three coins. One to three coin lots will receive placement in the main sections of the catalog and will receive photographs on our web site. Lots of four or more coins fall into the category called "Large Lots," which will be discussed next. Once again, the key point for you to remember here is that if your overall consignment is a good one, you may be able to negotiate a more lenient lot and photography standard.

- Work out the best arrangement to sell your "Large Lots" profitably. Remember the rolls of "Wheat pennies" you accumulated by date and mintmark over the years? How about the five proof sets you ordered from the Mint each year for the last three decades? Or the cheaper coins that you religiously stapled into 2 by 2s and stored in fourteen different stock boxes... sound familiar? We understand that all of these purchases contributed to your collecting pleasure, but we have one question to ask... would you travel somewhere else in the country to buy them today? The answer is almost certainly, "no," and that answer applies to virtually everyone else as well. As discussed previously, it is the "cream" of a collection that is most likely to "overperform" at a major auction. Large lots are at the other end of the spectrum. It's a matter of logistics. By their very nature, large lots are bulky, cumbersome to carry to auction sites and heavy to ship once sold. They are time-consuming to catalog and require a lot of extra effort to earn the same percentage as a single coin of comparable lot value. Auction company personnel are not very fond of the large lots in major auctions and neither are most bidders, because their focus is on the more "high-powered" lots. Auctioneers will take your large lots for a big sale, but you have absolutely no leverage and that's not what auctions are all about! In most cases, you would be better off asking the auctioneer to bid the large lots straight up. You will probably realize greater net proceeds and get paid immediately. Our company has an additional option. We put on "large lot only" sales. They're not fancy and the lots don't get any kind of extensive write-ups. What they do get is a bidder base of the country's strongest buyers of large lot material. These are dealers who specialize in (relatively) inexpensive coins, sets and bulk. We know who they are and they're fiercely competitive. We've been inviting them to our offices about two to three times annually for the last decade to buy the remnants of our collection purchases and are frequently amazed at what we get. Now we're taking consignments and letting the public in on this "well kept" secret! You do have to wait a bit longer for auction and settlement than with an outright sale, but it can be well worth it!

Occasionally, people ask us why they shouldn't dispose of their coins to or through a collector. The premise, of course, is that the collector would pay more and the playing field would be more level. There is some general merit to those statements, but there are some caveats as well.

- A collector will pay more for some coins, but will rarely pay more for all the coins. Take care that you don't get a bit more for the best few pieces of your collection only to find that nobody wants what's left.

- Being a collector in and of itself is no guarantee that the individual you contact is any more or less knowledgeable or moral than a dealer. We think on average, dealers would be better informed on current market conditions, upgrade potential and the reputations of potential buyers. We know of at least one situation where a collector acquaintance sold a collection for heirs, only to take a bad check from the buyer. That individual was well known as a "bad egg" by the dealer community, but the collector/agent was totally unaware. It took more than a year and considerable expense for the heirs to collect a fraction of what was owed.

- As an agent, the collector is less likely to have insurance coverage for your collection while in his care. If you use a collector, don't forget to verify this just as you would with a dealer.

The bottom line is that you should qualify a collector in the same manner as you would a dealer. While you may see some advantages in such a relationship, don't overlook dealer advantages that you may be taking for granted.

The final issues of etiquette are the relationships between a collector and his heirs, and between the heirs themselves. The collector, as the owner, has all the rights and responsibilities for the collection in his lifetime, and can provide guidance (or not) to his heirs as he sees fit. That said, any guidance (as opposed to none) is often a blessing. Even if only one or a portion of the heirs has any interest in the coins, a general understanding by all where they fit into the picture goes a long way towards familial harmony. The collector should identify and detail specific bequests if that is desirable. "Dad split them up that way in the will" is a lot more powerful than "I'm sure Dad wanted me to have this one." Similarly, the collector should indicate who should be contacted to help dispose of the collection... and who should not! It's amazing how many "old friends" can appear after the death of a known collector. The Executor, be he or she a family member or not, should be advised of all these details.

Heirs should remember that the other heirs are also probably under a great deal of stress, so be considerate of each other. We like to think that family is the most important thing, so here are some tips to avoid controversy if the collection needs to be split or disposed of equitably when specific guidance was not provided.

Leave the division to a third party. If the collection is not to be sold, have the appraiser break the inventory into the appropriate number of groups by value. If one or more heirs want specific pieces, have the appraiser value those individually and if the remainder of the collection is sold, use those amounts to adjust shares accordingly. Finally, if the collection is to be disposed of, but each heir wants "something" to remember the deceased by, determine the dollar value you want set aside and have each heir "buy" the coin(s) they want at the appraised price.. In all cases, remember to keep things in perspective. The coins once provided a great deal of pleasure to your loved one, and if there is any sentiment to be attached to them, it should be a positive one!

This has been a difficult handbook to prepare. There are two main reader groups, neither of whom should be happy at the implications of needing to read it. If you are a collector, the thought of estate planning may make you look closer at your own mortality than you wanted to. If a current heir, you've probably read this because your loved one declined to face that reality and left you a burden along with the inheritance.

We would take more pleasure in relating a more upbeat subject, but will be satisfied if this handbook has made things a little easier for you in addressing a difficult task. In closing, we offer this final guidance regardless of your circumstance or role:

1. Determine what your goal is.

2. Know your options.
3. Analyze them and pick the best course of action for you.

4. Make a plan.

5. If you need assistance, choose it carefully.

6. Above all, remain flexible and don't be afraid to adjust your plan as you go along.

Good Luck!

APPENDICES

APPENDIX A – NUMISMATIC
FRATERNAL ORGANIZATIONS

American Numismatic Association (ANA)
818 North Cascade Avenue
Colorado Springs, CO 80903
1-719-632-2646
FAX 1-719-634-4085
E-mail: ana@money.org
Web site: www.money.org

The American Numismatic Association is the country's largest
collector organization for coins and related items. Formed in 1891, the
ANA offers educational programs, an authentication service (no grading),
and a monthly magazine, *The Numismatist*. Its Colorado Springs
headquarters features a first-rate museum and library that are available to
members and non-members alike. The ANA offers renowned summer
seminars on a number of numismatic subjects and holds two conventions
annually. These shows offer 250 to 500 bourse tables and significant
auctions. The annual convention auction (held in July or August) is
frequently the best grossing auction sale of the year.

Professional Numismatists Guild (PNG)
3950 Concordia Lane
Fallbrook, CA 92028
1-760-728-1300
FAX 1-760-728-8507
E-mail: info@pngdealers.com
Web site: www.pngdealers.com

The Professional Numismatists Guild is the preeminent dealer group
in the coin industry. Formed in 1955 with the motto, "Knowledge,
Integrity, Responsibility," the PNG accepts members only after stringent
background and financial investigations, and a vote of the entire
membership. Members agree to uphold a strict code of ethics and to
resolve any complaints against them through binding PNG arbitration.
Lists of PNG dealers are available from the organization.

Continued on next page

American Numismatic Society (ANS)

Broadway at 155th Street
New York, NY 10032
212-234-3130
FAX: 1-212-234-3381
E-mail: info@amnumsoc.org
Web site: www.amnumsoc.org

The American Numismatic Society was founded in 1858, and is dedicated to the serious study of numismatic items. To that end, they have an extensive research library and world-class collections, and provide members and visiting scholars with a broad selection of publications, topical meetings and symposia, fellowships and grants, honors and awards, and various educational projects. Membership information can be obtained at their website or by telephone. The ANS hopes to be moved into their new location during 2001, so call for latest information regarding location and visiting hours.

APPENDIX B – INSURANCE COMPANIES
Offering NUMISMATIC COVERAGE

Cleland & Associates
P O Box 899
Galveston, TX 77553-0899
1-409-766-7101
FAX: 1-409-766-7102
Contact: Richard Cleland

North American Collectibles Association
2316 Carrollton Road
Westminster, MD 21157
1-800-685-6746
1-410-857-5011
FAX 1-410-857-5259
Contact: Barbara Wingo
E-mail: nacabdw@aol.com

Woller, Seabury & Smith
1440 N. Northwest Highway
Park Ridge, IL 60068-1400
1-800-323-2106
1-847-803-3100

Hugh Wood, Inc.
(American Agent for Lloyds of London)
45 Broadway, 3rd Floor
New York, NY 10006
1-212-509-3777
FAX: 1-212-509-4906
Contact: Jack Fisher

APPENDIX C – THIRD-PARTY GRADING SERVICES

Numismatic Guaranty Corporation (NGC)
P O Box 1776
Parsippany, NJ 07054
1-973-515-4000
FAX: 1-973-599-9291

A N A C S
P O Box 182141
Columbus, OH 43218
1-800-888-1861
FAX: 1-614-791-9103
Web Site: www.anacs.com

Professional Coin Grading Service (PCGS)
P O Box 9458
Newport Beach, CA 92658
1-800-447-8848
1-949-833-0600
FAX: 1-949-833-7660

Independent Coin Grading (ICG)
7901 E. Belleview Avenue, Ste. 50
Englewood, CO 80111
1-877-221-4424
1-303-221-4424
FAX: 1-303-221-5524
E-mail: customersatisfaction@icgcoin.com

NOTES

NOTES

FREE
Fair Market Value Appraisal

This certificate entitles you, your estate executor or heir to a no-cost, no-obligation appraisal of your numismatic collection. This written appraisal may either be a current total valuation, or total value at the time of transfer (for estate, tax, or family purposes).

Heritage Numismatic Auctions, Inc.
Attn: Estate Services
100 Highland Park Village, 2nd Floor
Dallas, TX 75205-2788
1-800-872-6467   FAX: 214-528-2596
www.HeritageCoin.com

FREE
Additional
Information and Updates

☐ Please send me info on your new FREE Coin Collector Inventory Computer Program!

☐ Please send me additional information on rare coin estate planning.

☐ Please send me annually updated information through "The Rare Coin Estate Newsletter."

Name_____

Address_____

City_____ ST_____ ZIP_____

Phone: Day:_____ Night:_____

Fax:_____

Email:_____

Heritage Numismatic Auctions, Inc.
Attn: Estate Services
100 Highland Park Village, 2nd Floor
Dallas, TX 75205-2788
1-800-872-6467   FAX: 214-528-2596
www.HeritageCoin.com

Heritage Numismatic Auctions, Inc.
Attn: Estate Services
100 Highland Park Village, 2nd Floor
Dallas, TX 75205-2788
1-800-872-6467   FAX: 214-528-2596
www.HeritageCoin.com